REDROCK ALMANAC

Redrock Almanac

Canyon Country Vignettes

Johnson Books
Boulder

Linked by terrain, mission, and purpose, members of Peaks, Plateaus & Canyons Association (PPCA) collaborate to promote understanding and stewardship of the Colorado Plateau. PPCA supports and fosters professionalism among member organizations through cooperation in mutually beneficial projects, networking, and training.

Published by Johnson Books, a Big Earth Publishing company,
3005 Center Green Drive, Suite 220, Boulder, Colorado 80301.
E-mail: books@bigearthpublishing.com
www.bigearthpublishing.com
1-800-258-5830

Cover and text design by Melissa Guy

9 8 7 6 5 4 3 2 1

Library of Congress Cataloging-in-Publication Data
Engelhard, Michael, 1959-
Redrock almanac: canyon country vignettes / by Michael Engelhard.
    p. cm.
  ISBN 1-55566-395-8
  1. Natural history—Colorado Plateau. 2. Colorado Plateau. I. Title.
  QH104.5.C58E537 2006
  508.791'3—dc22   2006035777

Printed in China

ACKNOWLEDGMENTS

My work on several anthologies taught me one thing: it may take only a single person to conceive an idea but many are needed to bring it to fruition. Among those who made *Redrock Almanac* not only possible but also stunning are the following photographers: John Blaustein, Bob Cameron, Lynn Chamberlain, James Crotty, Dean Cully, Kevin Ebi, Melissa Hutchison, Joel D. Lusk, Steve MacAulay, Tony Markle, Markus Mauthe, Suzi Moore McGregor, Mike Morrison, H. Scott Page, Andrew Reitsma, and John Running. Thanks to each of you for lending your vision and for indulging a canyon rat with a limited budget and never-ending string of requests. Tom Till in Moab particularly deserves my gratitude for donating over thirty photos from his extensive archives, which make up the visual bulk of this book. Lata Shambo assisted the project with photo editing. I am indebted to Melissa Guy for expertly packaging these words and images. (Here's to intelligent design!) She contributed photos as well and is a companion with inexhaustible patience. Despite forbidding production costs, Mira Perrizo of Johnson Books saw the niche for a Colorado Plateau pictorial with a different format and angle and acted promptly—no mean feat in these times of bottom-line publishing. Don Montoya, Scott Thybony, and especially Diane Allen and Christa Sadler were invaluable in helping me get the facts straight. Any errors that remain are mine alone. The United States Geological Survey provided a fine map for the book. Richard Pennington cleaned up my prose, a job seldom seen. Final thanks go to Cindy Hardgrave of the Canyonlands Natural History Association, who gave me the opportunity to cut my writer's teeth on this haiku-like genre in the association's calendars.

CONTENTS

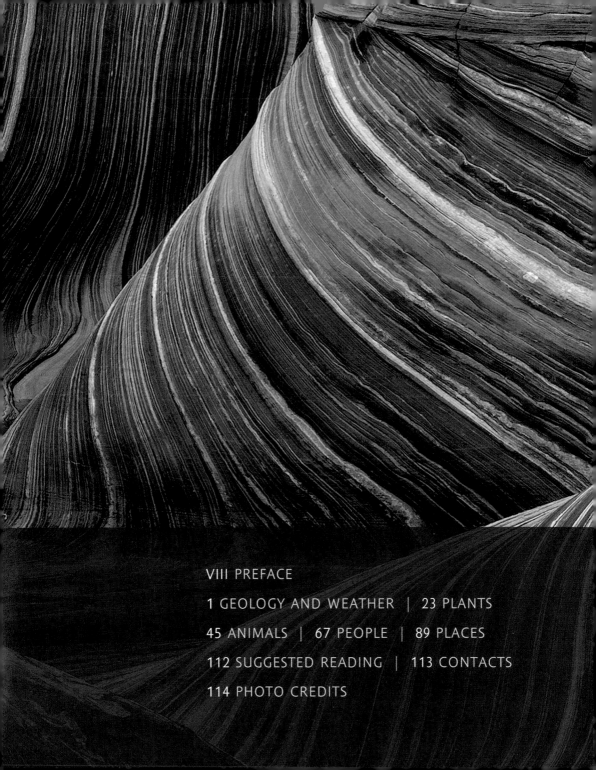

PREFACE

The newcomer's complaint about a lack of true seasons on the Colorado Plateau is unwarranted. Upon closer acquaintance, its perennial displays are likely to shock the senses.

MANY PEOPLE "KNOW" the Colorado Plateau's mesas and buttes, its hoodoos, arches, corroded plains, and corkscrew gashes from John Ford's Westerns, cigarette commercials, or personal experience. And yet, one lifetime is too short to explore its hidden abundance, to fully grasp the nuances and moods of this place.

On a satellite image the plateau stands out as a well-defined oval wrinkled by large river systems—the old face of Earth itself. But its contours dissolve with proximity as soon as the visitor leaves pavement to wander through sandstone mazes. The home of coyotes and wrens absorbs busloads of tourists each year. It seduces with surreal scenery, with dust-devil antics, with sun-baked space that resists occupation. Its ruggedness and seclusion defy cartographic abstraction. Aridity saved it from dense settlement. On any road map, towns appear scattered about as mere afterthoughts. A slew of colors outline national parks, forests, monuments, wilderness areas, Bureau of Land Management and tribal lands in a hodgepodge managed by entities with conflicting agendas. The artificial boundaries of four states dissect what should be indivisible, perhaps even sacred. Survey lines draw together arbitrarily near Monument Valley's skyline—in a region known as the Four Corners—zeroing in on the Navajo Nation's spiritual hub. The modern grid clashes with roundness, with healing mandalas, stone calendars, drums, sheep corrals, and earth dwellings banked up like anthills. It clashes with philosophies of the universe that strive for harmony. It clashes with organic forms: birds' and rodents' nests, rainbows, river meanders, coiled serpents, the sun's trajectory. The confrontation challenges some people to ignore and transcend self-imposed limitations. Others cling to guidebooks or itineraries. But wonder cannot be contained. Mystery cannot be reduced to a three-starred attraction. Only those who cross lines are able to meet this reticent land on its own terms.

We stand to gain much by abandoning the blurred vantage of highways. Leaving behind fenced-off viewpoints, we become free to venture into the heart of heat and emptiness. We find that the sand-colored stillness deceives. It rewards the curious with conundrums and discoveries, with memories and insights unlikely to fade with time. A menagerie of desert creatures scurries about, concealed by darkness or tawny skins. Tracks stitch the mud linings of waterholes, telling eloquent stories. Birds as garish as the spectrum of stratified stone flit through gallery forests. From dagger-leafed agaves at the Grand Canyon's bottom to box elder groves, from silver-slick aspens to lichen-encrusted boulders in the Abajo, La Sal, or Henry mountains, this physiographic province allows travelers to sample six life zones—equivalent to those bracketing Mexico and Canada—in less than a day and without a passport.

The newcomer's complaint about a lack of true seasons on the Colorado Plateau is unwarranted. Upon closer acquaintance, its perennial displays are likely to shock the senses. Spring's verdure succumbs to summer's yellow brittleness punctuated by downpours, deluges of biblical intensity that briefly cleanse the brooding air. Heralding the monsoon months, flash floods run amok in drought-wracked expanses. Soon wildflower starbursts yield to the autumnal russet of scrub oaks. Before we have had our fill of color or scent, temperatures plunge below freezing, frosting cacti and rocks. Claret cup blossoms wear caps of confectionary sugar. Pothole ice cracks under our steps like fine china. All the drama and spectacle mix in a paradoxical and at times treacherous mélange, a cocktail that can hit the uninitiated ill-prepared and leave them reeling.

The geology dazzles with equal eccentricity. Between the brindled flanks of Canyon de Chelly and Bryce Canyon's peek-a-boo world, countless works of "natural art" await connoisseurs willing to risk dehydration. Rock spans, alcoves, "petrified" dunes, eroded scarps, hogbacks, basalt pillars, and limestone reefs bring to mind windowless skyscrapers, subway tunnels, fairy factories, battleships, mega-mushrooms, cloud plantations, or fever dreams. Slowly, we realize: not every mirage dissolves at a hiker's approach.

Despite the rough edges of this landscape, there is solace in knowing that you can learn to flow with it. Time spent here ultimately translates into a literacy of place. Game trails avoid most trouble spots as they cross the billowing terrain. Cottonwood green leads you to hidden waters. And the angle of rock strata suggests escape routes from routines into box canyons.

The wealth of this best-of-beyond lies as much in its human heritage as in its natural splendor. Our civilization's backyard has always drawn fringe dwellers. Slave traders, trappers, desperados, adventurers, immigrants, missionaries, and miners thirsted for bounties, pelts, other folks' livestock, unfettered country, freedom of religion, souls, or gold. But when colonial powers first claimed this "wilderness," it had long been cultivated. A veneer of stories already sheathed the land. Pre-Columbian societies recorded the things that centered and grounded them, by scratching glyphs into rock patinas. They inhabited multi-tiered cliff fortresses at Mesa Verde, Keet Seel, and Betatakin. Trade networks and the exchange of ideas far predated European arrivals. For centuries, observations of celestial movements had been fine tuned. Roads linked Chaco Canyon's metropolis with outlier communities as far flung as Casas Grandes south of what would later become the Mexican border. Echoes of aboriginal primogeniture linger in Hopi banded pottery designs, as they do in blankets radiant with mineral and plant dyes from the Navajo homeland Dinétah. Present-day pilgrimages to salt mines in the Grand Canyon or masked dancers stomping mesa dust, summoning rain to the buzzing of rattles and flutes, stem from the same archaic traditions. Such residue also yields grist for the mill of contemporary longings. Pueblo Bonito. Bisti Badlands. Shiprock. Rainbow Bridge. Kayenta. Cortez. Panguitch.... Spoken like mantras and in different tongues, sonorous names conjure the land's bastard heritage. They entice dreamers with visionary geographies. The spellbound seek tranquility, new directions, a simpler life, or excitement, and very few leave disappointed. Many spend weeks, even months, on the Colorado Plateau. Some stay for good, in the end adding their bones to those already enriching the ground.

Redrock Almanac is my attempt to distill the essence of a hardscrabble land—for those who have yet to find their way there, as well as for those already changed by previous encounters. The following pages are peepholes rather than windows; they offer glimpses instead of clichéd views or postcard scenery. Despite the old saw that a picture says more than a thousand words, I understand image and text as complementary, equally valid forms of expression. The art of photography captures the high desert's hues, its shapes, textures, and forever-evanescent light. It fixes the glint in a raven's eye with the same truthfulness as a mountain lion's backlit whiskers. These are details that largely resist description. By contrast, words widen the focus, providing background and access to nonvisual perceptions. They expose relationships and, even more importantly, dependencies. Both perspectives weave into the reflection of an extraordinary landscape, a changing landscape, a landscape threatened by too many demands.

The almanac entries that trace vanished civilizations serve as mementos, reminders of our transient tenure in a country blessed with deep time and little rain. Beyond that they uphold the promise of lives in alignment with nature. Ultimately the book in your hands is a plea to identify with places close to home, to ensure that plants and animals, landforms and rivers, but especially silence and the sublime will outlast our depictions of them.

GEOLOGY AND WEATHER

According to cliché, mystery can be found in a grain of sand.
Even more so, it can be found in windblown grains of sand.

Schist

ALMOST TWO BILLION YEARS ago the ocean floor was being forced under North America's more buoyant continental crust. The ongoing collision mangled the ancient seabed, an arc of volcanic islands, and parts of both tectonic plates. Far below the surface, searing pressure and heat welded these remnants together. Thus Vishnu schist was born—a resilient metamorphic rock as dark as night. Clarence Dutton—one of John Wesley Powell's geologists—named the Grand Canyon's buttes, which in turn lent their names to three distinct schists: Rama, Vishnu, and Brama. Of this Hindu trinity, Vishnu is the god responsible for preserving the world's workings.

Eons after its creation the superimposed layers had worn away, baring this Precambrian foundation like roots in a cutbank. The grandfather of rocks crops up in only two locations on the Colorado Plateau. One is the Grand Canyon's inner gorge, the other a river section between the Colorado state line and town of Moab known as Westwater Canyon.

Downstream of the Cisco Ranger Station the Colorado River constricts into a frothing maw. Red Wingate cliffs capping the schist recede, making room for a fractured yet polished seam, a lining much harder than sandstone and consequently more resistant to erosion. Jet-black walls absorb sunlight intense enough to spark cactus blossoms or blister bare feet. The stream starts to hurry here, bent on breaking the boulders that spike its channel. A dirty dozen of rapids drones in the narrows ahead. The Staircase. Funnel Falls. Bowling Alley. Sock-it-to-me. Last Chance.... Despite their jaunty names, on a gloomy day the setting can intimidate even experienced boatmen.

Skull Rapid foams through Westwater's tightest bottleneck, the crux of the entire run. While I prepare for my turn by strapping down gear I take in the fluted schist, walls that threaten to converge in front of the raft. Two fangs lurk halfway down this rapid: Clam Rock and Razor Rock. Here the unwary can truly get caught between a rock and a hard place. It takes a tricky rowing maneuver to avoid both obstacles and keep boats from flipping or from having their bellies ripped open. As the impatient current grabs my bow I pray to Vishnu to redeem me once again.

Sandstone

THE MOAB REGION is famous among canyon aficionados for its large number of natural arches, including even a few double and triple spans, which open like windows into the geological past. Contrary to the Old Norse origin of *window* (from "wind-eye") and the belief of novices to the Colorado Plateau, wind is *not* the main force responsible for crafting these portals into the blue yonder. Water alone whittled the incredible array of arches, fins, spires, and balanced rocks from the desert's raw materials. Some 200 million years of sandblasting merely honed contours to an exquisite finish emphasizing the work of frost and flood.

Ancient winds *did*, however, lend a hand in the deposition of sand. Jurassic dune fields as far away as Oregon gave birth to the ivory and salmon borders that hem in many canyons. Piled layer upon layer, volatile sands melded under pressure and chemical bonding into the Southwest's emblematic rock strata. In Zion National Park the deposits measure thousands of feet in thickness.

Erosion never sleeps, and abraded particles from the sandstone and shale formations typical of the plateau affect the hiker's life in many ways. Airborne, the nearly indestructible quartz crystals rake and sting faces and hands before they sift into gullies or bury boulders. Dunes accumulate on the lee side of rocky ridges, miring down weary backpackers. On stormy days a ruddy dust colors creeks and bushes, my hair, the wind, and sunsets. I wear it like a second skin. It adds fiber to foods, tints the pages of my notebook, my gear, and at times even my dreams. Quite frequently a chocolate-colored sludge is the only potable water. Untreated, this concoction is too thick to drink and too insubstantial to shape into pottery. But I grit my teeth anyway, imbibe the good earth and truly partake of the essence of place. Some backcountry travelers consider the sediment-laden water dirty or polluted. I remind them that the dangerous stuff is usually what you cannot see or taste.

Waterfalls

ALTHOUGH I FEEL TEMPTED to stop at the pictograph panel or reed-rimmed beaver ponds, I hurry toward the commotion at the head of the box canyon. In the shade of tall cottonwood trees five or six photographers have set up tripods, waiting for sunlight to graze the rim. The focus of their attention is Lower Calf Creek Falls, the Colorado Plateau's most-photographed cascade. From a V-shaped notch in the Navajo sandstone skeins of white unravel 126 feet into a pool at the alcove's bottom. Spray hisses against moss-slick abutments, glazing them with mineral residue. Mist curtains the gorge, contributing to its cool, green ambience. Black rocks litter the pool's crescent beach like the lustrous eggs of some mythical bird. The current trundled them from lava beds on the Aquarius Plateau—seven miles to the north—that girdle Calf Creek's headwaters.

Like springs and seeps, waterfalls create oases in arid landscapes. Shade-loving maidenhair fern and columbines thrive in their moist environments. Nutrients and topsoil from upstream are deposited below the falls' drops, allowing dogwood, box elders, and willows to gain footholds. These plants in turn attract wildlife, ranging from garter snakes to mule deer. Most falls in Canyon Country, and by extension the biodiversity they foster, owe their existence to the mechanics of erosion. A streamlet like Calf Creek that hurtles across a plateau to rendezvous with a larger river—in this case the Escalante—digs its canyon more slowly than does the main watercourse. At the junction it often ends in a hanging valley, a stair step between tributary and river corridor requiring a leap to the lower level. Volcanic intrusions can cause a less common type of cataract, like the Grand Falls of the Little Colorado River. When cooling lava dams a streambed, water will try to bypass or jump such a hurdle.

I wade past the gauntlet of photographers, waist-deep into Calf Creek's aquamarine pool. While I enjoy a close-up view and pinpricks of cold, the artists take a well-deserved break.

Chert

AFTER MILES OF cottonwood-lined meanders the creek wiggles through a narrows of Hermosa Group strata. Here water unearthed and buffed tiers of bluish limestone—sidewalks studded with chert nodules. Southeastern Utah's Jasper Canyon was named for a variety of the mineral, and ancient civilizations knew those deposits as a source for weapons and tools.

Chert occurs in a wide range of colors, including white, brown, green, yellow, black, red, and sometimes even a mix of several. Its names are equally plentiful: flint, onyx, agate, bloodstone, and chalcedony. Red chert, or jasper, derives its intense color from iron oxide. Dissolved minerals carried by water frequently aggregate in rock pockets, forming the crystal lenses typical of the sediment formation on which I walk. Chert can also build up when the exoskeletons of microscopic marine organisms bond under pressure at an ocean's bottom. Tightly interlocking quartz crystals give this rock its great density, luster, and razor edges. Due to its homogeneity the glassy material flakes nicely under pressure, and it is said that chert blades can be sharp enough to shave with.

To my delight I come upon a slickrock shelf above the creek that is inlaid with splinters of chert. Cleared of sand by water and wind the scatter has aligned into desert pavement intaglio. Many fragments remain embedded in chunks of the mother rock, which resemble raisin bread loaves. Fingernail- to fist-size pieces shine like fresh meat or have the marbled sheen and heft of petrified wood. Walking around, I detect slivers that have clearly been worked. Concentric pressure ridges are tell-tale signs on these flakes. The raw material for lithic ("stone") tools was coveted throughout the pre-Columbian Southwest, only equaled in value by turquoise, paint pigments, or seashells. Skilled hunters devised a variety of designs for blades, points, arrowheads, burins, scrapers, and adzes, to meet specialized needs. They struck cores for implements from lumps of chert and refined them with the tine of a deer antler or similar utensil. I wonder whether bloodstone—resembling the juice of life—held hunting magic for them.

Monsoon Season

THE VIOLENT MONSOON SEASON of July and August stuns many visitors to the Colorado Plateau. In their dualistic view of the universe, the resident Navajos (or Diné) perceive gentle spring rains as female, bearing fertility, tickling crops into sprouting. Sometimes dryness sucks up this drizzle before it can reach the ground. The fierce male rains of late summer—unleashed during thunderstorms—are its complement and polar opposite. Followed by flash floods they flay the land, stripping it of its cover.

While summer mornings initially beckon with baby-blue innocence, cumulus clouds may creep up on canyon rims, piling on top of each other, boiling, blossoming, and slowly assuming the dull gray of slate. Before hikers can find shelter in alcoves or under trees, heaven's spillways open in a release that pounds cottonwood canopies and rattles box elder leaves. Thunder and lightning rend a sullen sky; rock corridors rumble like the bowling alleys of titans. But lightning-sparked wildfires help rejuvenate desert vegetation, and species like the ponderosa pine cannot even propagate without them.

Rounding the bend of a gulch, one may witness a spectacle rare in its transience. Rain sheeting off tablelands has been funneled into increasingly deeper grooves. Soon, water spouts from every rimrock cleft, fanning out in graceful arcs before splattering and vaporizing upon impact hundreds of feet below. Mist billows over plunge pools. Frenetic applause and foot stomping echo through the hollows. Cascades skip from ledge to ledge, streaking cliff faces. On talus slopes boulders sweat, and vegetation takes on tropical tints. Frequently the rain stops as abruptly as it began; but long after a gully washer, gorges keep ringing with the eloquence of water that tumbles from puckered plateaus.

As the sun splits clouds it turns canyons into greenhouses, filling them with earthy scents. Moisture drips from dense foliage. Curlicues of steam rise from the ground. Rows of drops cling to willows and bent reeds. With the slightest aftermath of wind they quiver and blink in prismatic colors. Entire constellations find room on a single leaf.

Potholes

AFTER THE RAINS of a week ago, puddles wink from slickrock terraces in The Maze, mirroring sky, clouds, and rock—the essentials. Morning light also catches in potholes near the canyon's bottom, creating miniature suns that burn at my feet. As a boon to being alone in the backcountry there is no need for table manners. A dying person crawling through the desert may sip the delicious fluid directly from the ground, like an animal at a waterhole. Above all, the "kissing" of puddles is practical: superficial draughts avoid stirring up algae and sediment, and bedrock depressions are often too shallow for dipping a cup.

Troughs perforating a canyon's course are signatures of currents long gone. Whirlpools and other hydraulics gouged them out by dissolving the cement that welds individual quartz grains into sandstone. River gravel got caught in them and—swirled about by the water's fretting—smoothed these pits, excavating them even more. Some are steep-sided or undercut, deep enough to trap unprepared canyoneers.

On a more benign note, potholes can be windows into fascinating worlds. The hiker who has stilled her thirst and takes time to look closely may feel a little like Alice at the rabbit hole. She will discover a bug-eat-bug world, teeming with backswimmers, predacious diving beetles, gyrating commas of mosquito larvae, tadpoles, and translucent fairy shrimp, ethereal as baubles of blown glass. Many of these organisms lie dormant during the long dry periods, surviving desiccation and extreme soil temperatures. As soon as a rain shower or flood fills a pothole, life bursts forth to multiply and mature as if on amphetamines. Red-spotted toads take only three days to slip from their gelatinous eggs. Within three weeks the tadpoles morph into adults. Tadpole shrimp—living fossils that look like undersized horseshoe crabs— require even less time to complete their cycle. Considerate backpackers never defile these quickly shrinking hatcheries as bathtubs. They take water only in emergencies and with a clean receptacle. Lip balm, sunscreen, or natural skin oils can pollute these microcosms, killing all their inhabitants.

Sand Dunes

WHEN I RETURN to camp the wash is adrift with sand. Sand accumulates in the lee of boulders and at the bases of bushes. Sand stings my calves. Sand pelts my pack. It peppers my tent. Inside, everything has been sifted over with a rust-red powder. It looks as if the desert were claiming ownership of my belongings.

The vocabulary of geographers glitters with terms for types of sand dunes borrowed from Turkish and Arabic languages: serir, reg, barchan, and seif—the latter describing a scimitar-shaped, sharp-crested dune. According to cliché mystery can be found in a grain of sand. Even more so it can be found in *windblown* grains of sand.

At high air velocities sandy patches begin to creep. Ripples seem to be swimming. Entire dunes start to migrate, their normally crisp outlines blurred. This is not just another delusion brought on by heat. Sand grains *do* hop and skitter along the ground like a plague of fleas, in a process known as saltation. Upon landing they crash into other grains, knocking them loose and forward, causing friction that accounts for the characteristic hissing. Once in motion they continue even when the wind slows down. Finer particles stay aloft and travel farther, as dust. Granules too heavy to be moved are left behind.

Mesozoic winds created the local Navajo sandstone. Tiring, they dropped airborne quartz crystals that accumulated into dunes and eventually bonded into laminated knolls and domes. These crystals are so resilient that some have made it through the mill of weathering, erosion, and deposition not just once but several times. Some sand always slides down the steep leeward slope or slipface of a dune. In this manner, the dune and even the tiniest ripples advance. The miniature avalanches also form distinct, wafer-thin planes that persist after a dune turns to stone. This onionskin texture of sandstone is called crossbedding; changes in its dips and slants tell of shifting wind directions in the paleo-environment. Quartz impurities created a rich palette of sands, many of which find use in Navajo sand paintings.

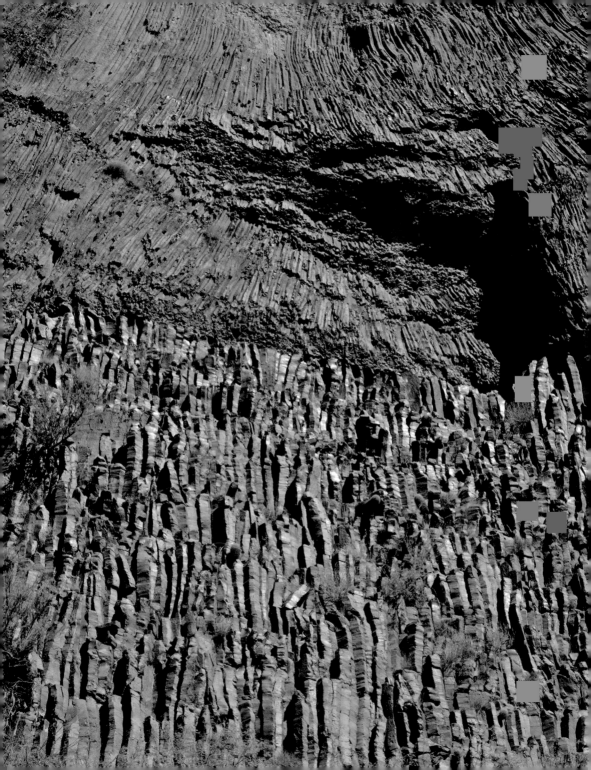

Volcanism

AS YOU DRIVE SOUTH from the Cameron trading post toward Flagstaff, cinder and ragged basalt replace the Painted Desert's rainbow shale. The land lies torched, disfigured with pustules and scabs like scrofulous skin. You are approaching the fiery rim of the Colorado Plateau. Several million years of volcanic activity even sculpted the snowbound range on the horizon. Geologists consider this region to be fickle and check the San Francisco Volcanic Field with seismographs, predicting new outbursts.

During several episodes lava from the Uinkaret Mountains and Toroweap area encroached upon the North Rim of the Grand Canyon. Slopping into the chasm, it blocked the Colorado's flow. Some of these igneous dams rose to more than 2,000 feet. But the river persisted, grinding its way through each subsequent dike, the last time roughly a million years ago. Vulcan's Throne and a sprinkling of lesser cones overlook the Big Ditch; they are the progeny of Earth's violent birthing.

Off the highway, Sunset Crater—now a national monument—proclaims one of the most recent eruptions. During the late fall or winter of A.D. 1064 1065, a fountain of fire sprang from the ground. The flare and attendant mushroom cloud were visible from the distant Hopi mesas. Terrified, the local Sinagua abandoned cornfields they had farmed for generations. Archaeologists have been able to determine the exact date of their exodus by analyzing growth rings from wooden roof beams that lay buried under detritus. Amazingly, a Hopi myth also chronicles the traumatic event. It ascribes the meltdown to a Kachina spirit who unwillingly set a mountaintop ablaze. Out-of-control flames eventually merged with the underground hearth of Masau'u, god of fire and death.

At the visitor center I finger samples from the planet's viscera. Chunks of obsidian—a cool, smooth volcanic glass—were highly valued trade goods, the raw material for spear points and arrowheads. Frothy emissions stiffened into pumice, as light and porous as fossilized sponges. I walk through the sintered rubble of clinker lava, visualizing the impact of volcanic bombs, magma that hardened into muscle-like hunks while airborne. Amid the evidence of a temperamental deity I come to accept destruction as creation's indispensable twin.

Slot Canyons

WHEN NATURE CREATED slot canyons she was practicing for her masterpiece, the Grand Canyon. That gash of the Colorado marks an extreme, but forces and principles are the same. The difference amounts to a matter of scale. The generic term *canyon* from Spanish *caño* (meaning "tube," or "channel") defines one and all. And yet, slots defy shorthand descriptions; they can only be gauged with the body serving as yardstick.

In Earth's timeframe most slots are fledglings. They form as rapidly as anything geological can. They cleave the Wingate and Navajo sandstones and less frequently limestone, which is much harder. Kaibab limestone sheets most of the southern Colorado Plateau, and fewer slot canyons incise its surface. As tendrils of sudden precipitation follow joints and fissures in the rock—probing, prodding, jostling, prying, and harrowing—water finds lower levels but never rests. It enlists quartz grains and pebbles, occasionally even boulders, to do the handiwork of eternity. Entire sections of wall weaken and slough off; rubble is sluiced and sorted in a hurry. Yet it all happens too quickly for erosion of the flanks to keep up. In the end, entrenching always outpaces the widening.

Where withered earth offered itself to the impatience of water, its flesh has split open. Only the experienced and well equipped should enter, always mindful of the weather's fickleness.

It is cool inside, and a musty smell fills the timeworn passages. I spread-eagle to descend to the next level. One hand and one foot push at each wall, keeping the vise from closing. Where the angle strays from the vertical, I have to bend like a limbo dancer to follow the lead of stone. Stagnant potholes bar my way. The first letting go is the greatest challenge. As I ease into frigid, tea-colored water a breath catches high in my chest. The dank corridor is too narrow for full-fledged breaststrokes. I roll onto my back instead and focus on the ribbon of sky fluttering beyond reach. Choke stones and tree trunks are wedged fist-in-glove way above my head. They are the business cards of killer floods that rampage through these canyons at a moment's notice during the months of July and August.

Winter

"AFTER WE HAD GONE three leagues, we were stopped for a long time by a strong blizzard and tempest consisting of rain and thick hailstones amid horrendous thunderclaps and lightning flashes. We recited the Virgin's litany...." The following day, November 6, 1775, the Dominguez Escalante expedition forded the Colorado River in Glen Canyon. The padres had ventured from Santa Fé, seeking an overland route to California. But the onset of winter in early October near Sevier Lake, with cold winds and snowfall "so heavy that not only the sierra's heights but even all the plains were covered with snow," had driven them to abandon their mission and veer south.

Due to its high elevation, much of the Colorado Plateau qualifies as a "cold desert." While Indian summer often lingers into November, frost can descend for 180 days of the year. Temperatures may rocket from freezing to above 100°F during one day, and daily snowfalls of eight inches have been recorded for Moab. As moisture turns to ice, it expands in hairline cracks, wedging apart sandstone and accelerating erosion. Potholes lie cellophane-wrapped as the tension of water becomes visible in its freezing patterns. You can hear it stepping near the edges, a soft resonating "ping."

Winter drains color from the land, except for smudges of evergreen. The high desert looks alien now, its shapes grotesquely disguised, its barbs and spines softened by heavenly fluff. Canyons resound with the cawing of ravens. This is their lean season, but meals are always available from road kill or town dumpsters. Chickadees ruffle feathers to trap warmth. Migratory species head south, while lizards or snakes retreat underground. Beneath the brittle membranes of ponds beavers gnaw on a summer's savings: branches and twigs. Mourning cloak butterflies—the first to sunbathe each spring—winter in trunk hollows, sipping fermented tree sap. Deer mice curl up in woodpecker holes or, if homeless, become lethargic for much of the day to save calories. Life is on hold, rationing energy. These are lessons we could easily learn.

PLANTS

Like people who became adapted to hot, dry
environments, plants as well had to cope with the
desert's desiccating breath. Those that did not
became extinct.

Juniper

I AM READY to take a break, when—finally—a smoke tendril coils from the baseboard of my bow drill. After gently blowing on the punk I drop the ember into a nest from the fibrous bark of a juniper tree. It smolders there, fragile and fecund as a hummingbird egg. I keep aerating the tinder, trying not to inhale its pungency. The bark ignites, and I put it to my stack of dead branches, feeling a bit like Neanderthal man.

The uses of juniper are plenty, some as ancient as the human silhouettes on the wall that silently watch my efforts. Indigenous people of the Southwest harvested the bark to weave baskets, ropes, mats, sandals, and bags. The fuzzy outer filaments supplied material for diaper linings and menstrual pads. Healers rubbed the bark on spider bites, or collected gum from the evergreen tree to plug cavities in decayed teeth. The powder-blue berries, which really are wax-coated miniature cones, helped cure bladder infections. Diné toddlers wore necklaces of them to keep nightmares and evil spirits at bay. For the same reason, "singers" still burn juniper foliage during ceremonies. In more mundane applications straight sections become rot-resistant fence posts, while cones tenderize meat or flavor gin. Ash from the mineral-rich wood enhances cornmeal dishes, bread, or tamales.

But the corner store of canyon country also serves other-than-human customers. Its cones feed jackrabbits, coyotes, and winter-starved birds. Mule deer browse the twigs when snow buries other food sources.

The shaggy-skinned trees endure all this for a lifetime of up to 650 years. Their scaly leaflets decrease evaporation, enabling them to persevere in a dry, hot, *and* cold climate. Individual limbs may wither so that a tree can survive. Even sex has been pared down to a minimum. Utah junipers carry male flowers and berries on the same specimen at the same time, a mark of pioneer species that facilitates self-pollination.

As I breathe in the medicinal scent from my little fire, I thank these mesa-and-hillside ascetics. Together with their piñon pine brethren they make life in the desert livable.

Invasive Species

SPRINGTIME. THE CLOYING PERFUME of a tree with thorns and grayish leaves clogs the canyons. Its nondescript yellow flowers will soon transform into pitted seeds that resemble olives. Like tamarisk, Russian olive was introduced deliberately, around the 1850s, and for similar reasons: as windbreaks, as ornamentals, and to control erosion. But the plant escaped cultivation. It often replaces the same cottonwood trees it first seeks as neighbors. Fewer insects, fewer birds, fewer mammals find homes or sustenance in the rank thickets. As a result, many canyons have become quieter; some would say poorer. And yet, is the classification of a plant as "noxious" or "weed" not based upon *our* needs and preferences?

Downstream from Mineral Bottom, cottonwoods hold on to alluvial terraces and shade splendid campsites. But tamarisk belts block access by river runners as efficiently as barbed-wire fences. Park Service rangers and volunteers fight the curse of Southwestern gallery forests by cutting it down, poisoning it, or burning it. The most recent weapon in this protracted battle comes in the guise of yet another invited species—the Asian longhorn beetle that feeds on the pretty-in-pink-blooming bush. To ensure that the beetle itself will not turn into a pest, government agencies have conducted controlled release studies in Dinosaur National Monument and elsewhere.

Tumbleweed, the icon of Western freedom and desolation, is also nonnative to the Southwest. But the stowaway from Russian steppes is a perfect match for our windswept ranges, another rags-to-riches immigrant story. When Russian thistle matures it breaks loose from the disturbed soil it prefers. The skeleton bushes then bounce and roll as if possessed, until ditches or fences snag them. Numberless seeds are thus spread at the speed of a cantering horse. Within decades from its accidental introduction into South Dakota—mixed in with farmers' flax seeds—this transplant had conquered the intermountain West. For its affiliation with overgrazed prairies that marked westward expansion, the Hopi call tumbleweed White Man's Plant. Through the lens of history, unchecked humanity itself appears as an invasive species.

Adaptation

LIKE PEOPLE who became adapted to hot, dry environments—by means of dark skin pigments and additional sweat glands—plants as well had to cope with the desert's desiccating breath. Those that did not became extinct or prospered only in milder climes.

By downsizing surfaces and adjusting the shape of their leaves over time, Mormon tea, rabbitbrush, narrowleaf yucca, and others slowed down evaporation, which increases in windy conditions. Some evergreen trees obeyed the same principle, trading in broad leaves for needles. A waxy epidermis seals the foliage of manzanita and barberry bushes, thereby retaining moisture. Biennials hoard energy to flower only in alternating years, while whip-like Grand Canyon ocotillos do not invest in costly green before enough rain has fallen. Vegetation is naturally sparse on nutrient-poor desert soils, and some plants defeat competitors for life's elixir by secreting toxic chemicals. Members of the goosefoot family, like pickleweed, succeed through a higher tolerance of briny water, exuding excess salt to prevent cell damage.

But cacti are without doubt the masters of water conservation. They dispensed with leaves altogether, storing the chlorophyll that fuels photosynthesis entirely in succulent stems or pads. Their leaves devolved into spines, barbs, and glochids—fine bristles that irritate the lips of eager gourmets and break up moisture-sucking air currents.

Pale-skinned human transplants to the arid Southwest need to *learn* to compensate for the lack of adaptive physical traits. Smart people wear light-colored, loose clothing and broad-brimmed hats. The amount of water a hiker can carry often limits backpacking trips. I ration it accordingly, dry-brushing my teeth and using starchy leftover broth from boiled pasta as dishwater or to brew tea. Washing up is entirely out of the question, and after a week in the backcountry I am not sure if my mahogany tan is authentic.

Then there is the extended siesta, yet another behavioral modification. When the sun's bleak eye stares at me, I hide under piñons, rock overhangs, or a most-welcome cottonwood tree, imitating lizards by moving as little as possible.

Poison Ivy

WE PULL OUR RAFTS up on shore to check the shade of an overhang for a flat, sandy campsite. Due to the low water levels of past springs this camp has not been used in a while. A tangle of brush bars our way to the stream bench. My river-running companion who is bushwhacking ahead suddenly calls out, "Oh, no! Not again!" He rushes past me back to the river's edge where he frantically starts rinsing and rubbing his pale arms and legs. When I reach the place from which he bolted I locate the source of his dismay: a low bush sporting stalks with three glossy leaves each, burgundy-colored at this time of year, and chartreuse-veined. It takes only an instant to identify the obnoxious weed, this bane of hikers.

Strictly speaking, the shade- and moisture-loving member of the cashew family is not poisonous. Crushed or bruised, poison ivy leaves and stems secrete urushiol, a sticky, easily transferred and extremely stable compound that troubles some people but not others. The body absorbs and metabolizes this substance and often responds with an allergy. Itchiness, skin inflammation, and eventually clear blisters are the price reckless explorers pay. If it is not washed off within five minutes the oil can stay active on clothing and boots for up to a year. Simply touching contaminated clothes or gear can kindle a rash. Some herbalists who handled century-old specimens still contracted the plant's sting, and even the smoke of burning poison ivy can cause trouble.

But nature has a way of making up for much irritation she causes. Urushiol can be used to treat paralysis, arthritis, as a sedative, and—strangely enough—to cure certain skin disorders. Its sap dries into a black crust, yielding excellent ink and dye, or an ingredient for varnish. The off-white berries feed deer and songbirds during their fall migrations.

With one of our party cursing under his breath we untie and launch our boats once again, looking for more hospitable beaches downstream.

Alcove Garden

BEYOND THE CANYON'S first loop, time and weather have undermined the humped slickrock. Water trickles from the alcove's ceiling and walls, tumbles into a hollow thick with single leaf ash and Gambel's oak, and finally gathers in a dark, unassuming pool. A swath of sunlight falls onto nickel-sized tadpoles that squirm in the liquid, onto a golden-eyed frog whose flanks move in and out with each breath. Close by, a canyon wren practices descending scales. Minerals precipitate from the spring, wallpapering the back of the alcove chalk-white, gray, black, and rust; moisture glistens in places like paint running down an abstract canvas. Calcite deposits from constant seepage coarsen the rock. The twilight grotto amplifies dripping sounds into music, crystalline and sweet to a parched hiker.

Although water flowing from stone may strike some as pure sleight of hand, there is a natural explanation. Rain that saturates barren tablelands slowly filters through layers of sandstone. Where it encounters finer-grained, less porous material—such as siltstone or shale—groundwater follows this interface downhill until it gushes or leaks from canyon walls. In redrock country, springs and seeps often well from the dividing line between the Navajo and Kayenta formations. Alcove shade combines with abundant, year-round wetness into microhabitats not only for mammals, birds, amphibians, and insects, but for plants, many of which can only be found on the Colorado Plateau.

In this nook, as in others, perspiring cliffs created a hanging garden. Where the wall starts to slope, runoff has triggered a spurt of maidenhair fern. Droplets bead the plant's fronds, tresses that radiate an impossible green. Flowers nestle in soil pockets, quivering between water and light. Alcove columbines gleam in the recess, dainty and anemic as porcelain ballerinas. These relatives of the Colorado state flower blossom all summer, and their chalices outmatch all contenders in size. Petals of monkey flowers flash brilliant-red, quintuplet tongues lolling from tiny yellow throats. Death camas joins the frilled assembly in some gardens, reminding us of beauty's lethal side.

Piñons, People, and Jays

IN THE SAN RAFAEL SWELL the transition between civilization and wilderness comes as a swift awakening. I drop below the rim from a pullout on the interstate that dents upended rock strata like a giant's karate chop, leaving behind the sights and sounds and smells of pavement. After growling engines and clouds of diesel fumes, it feels refreshing to hike through clean-scented piñon and juniper forest, welcomed by the raucous chatter of jays.

Piñon jays live in symbiosis with *Pinus edulis*, the "edible pine"—New Mexico's state tree. Flocks numbering up to several hundred of the metallic-blue relatives of crows congregate in mixed coniferous woodlands. They constantly bicker while foraging, as a way to stay in touch and to warn each other of approaching predators. The birds feed almost exclusively on pine nuts, which they cache in leaf litter. Due to memory lapses they forget the locations of some. Widely distributed, the resulting seedlings do not compete with mature trees for water or sunlight but rather colonize new areas. Pines are slow-growing and do not tolerate extreme drought; they need all the help they can get. Jay populations fluctuate in sync with the abundance of piñon nuts, which peak every seven years. The hard-shelled tidbits are an important source of protein during spring nesting. When the nut crop is poor, the birds may delay breeding altogether until the next bumper crop. Tapping each shell to test for duds, a large flock can store up to a ton of nuts.

Native people have long been a strand in the weaving of tree and bird into the tapestry of life. They have gathered pine seeds in this region for at least 6,000 years. Diné women still collect nuts hidden by packrats and jays. Apologizing to the animal spirits, they leave behind snippets of tobacco or turquoise, as compensation and tokens of respect. Fall nut harvest was the time after which it became appropriate to while away nights around sputtering campfires. Elders recited sacred stories, beholding the world through their ancestors' eyes.

Sacred Datura

ANOTHER NOTORIOUS PLANT of the Canyon Country hides behind picturesque names: Thorn apple. Moonflower. Jimsonweed. Sacred datura. Native healers, wise in the uses of local fauna and flora, learned to tame its powers. They won an anesthetic by crushing the leaves and used it to treat sores and swellings, during the setting of bones, and to prevent miscarriages. In a strictly ritual context Paiute shamans, and fellow practioners in neighboring groups, drank a tea made from roots and seeds of the psychotropic weed. This libation induced hallucinogenic visions or trances. For hunting magic they sprinkled a powder from the ground-up roots into deer tracks and then prayed over them. The hexed animal would tire, lie down, and become easy prey.

This member of the potato family accumulates alkaloids from the soil, producing atropine, which serves as an antidote to the effects of nerve gas in chemical warfare. But at the same time—ingested in minute doses—the substance can cause giddiness, dimmed sight, stupefaction, blindness, and even death.

Datura's lurid corollas flare out between May and October. The trumpet-shaped moonflowers unfold only at night, announcing their availability to the sphinx moth—its nocturnal pollinator—with a heavy, extravagant scent reminiscent of lemons. Sphinx moths can become tipsy and uncoordinated while siphoning the flower's nectar. Blossoms wilt fast in the heat of day, in tender contrast to the golf-ball-sized prickly seedpods, the "thorn apples" resembling medieval weaponry or torture devices. The only insect impervious to a diet of the toxic leaves and stems is the striped datura beetle, a relative of the potato bug.

In one of my proudest feats as an outdoorsman I once identified a canyon by its scent alone. We were floating through Cataract Canyon, and the night was moonless, dark as the bottom of a stairwell. Dog-tired from the rapids and heat, we wanted to pull over at the mouth of Dark Canyon for a nap. I had hiked there before and recalled a pillow of datura near the canyon's mouth. Sure enough, a breeze soon carried the sultry perfume to our rafts.

Fremont Cottonwood

WHEN I SEEK cottonwood shade rather than sun I know that winter has once more surrendered to spring. The tree's dead branches, which I collect on occasion, burn not too hot and a bit smoky—passable fuel for summer campfires. When golden leaves dance in fall breezes with a motion and sound for which our language lacks words, I know that winter is about to return to the canyons.

Like the related willows, cottonwoods that form part of the original gallery forest of riparian zones prevent erosion and aerate soils, allowing water to filter downward. As drought shrinks the land, long taproots follow dropping groundwater tables, reaching for the hidden waters. At the same time they anchor saplings against flash floods and high winds. With their emerald leaves and furrowed trunks, mature trees point hikers to springs tucked into red rock crevices. They also provide nesting places for great blue herons, ravens, hawks, and occasionally even bald eagles. Songbirds mob their shivering canopies. Unfortunately, up to ninety percent of all cottonwood groves have by now fallen victim to livestock grazing, road construction, dam building, and—most of all—to introduced and resilient tamarisks or "salt cedars."

Fremont cottonwoods grow up to ninety feet tall, and rotted-out dead specimens can easily turn into "widow makers" during a storm. But their tenacity inspires. Reproducing not merely from seeds, new trees can also sprout from stumps, root crowns, or stem cuttings. Stately patriarchs and matriarchs bear male and female flowers respectively, exemplifying the complementary nature of even the plant world. Each spring white "cotton" tufts resembling shorn lambs' wool blanket the ground, which explains the tree's name. Part of it also honors a nineteenth-century western explorer, John C. Fremont.

Perhaps by observing beavers Native Americans throughout the Colorado Plateau learned to eat the cambium or inner bark to prevent scurvy. Pueblo Indians still fashion drums and Kachina dolls from the light, soft wood. Their Diné neighbors used it for fire drills, weaving loom frames, snowshoes, and cradleboards.

Yucca

WITH A PENKNIFE I sever one stiletto leaf from the rosette bristling at ground level. My students watch me pound it between rocks to soften the tough cuticle. Then I strip away the pulp, using the dull edge of my knife. Only yellowish plant fibers are left, connected by the spiny tip that juts from every yucca leaf. "Voila," I beam. "Your backcountry sewing kit." Impressed with the plant's handiness, the students want to hear more.

So far on this hike the group has paid attention exclusively to the yucca's spikes heavy with bloom. Blossoms droop in the heat, but splay each night to receive visitors. They are real showstoppers. Silky, cream-colored bells cluster around straight stems, like wax dripping from candelabra. Hence the evergreen's Spanish name: Our Lord's Candles. Mexican Catholics value the stalks as walking staffs for pilgrimages. But the uses of yucca vary across cultures and time. Ancestral Puebloans of the Four Corners split and chewed the leaves to make rope, sandals, baskets, matting for temporary shelter, and brushes to paint pictographs and pottery. The juicy buds and young flower stalks were covered with coals and roasted for hours or boiled; they taste like asparagus. My female students are especially interested in yucca's role during a Diné girl's coming-of-age ceremony. For this, elders peel, boil, and mash the roots of soap-tree yucca. Then they wash the young woman's hair with the suds, giving it an obsidian luster.

Lest we get too enthralled with the usefulness of things for humans, I talk about one of nature's dances of give-and-take. All species of Southwestern yucca evolved in close relationship with their pollinators, nocturnal moths of the genus *Pronuba*. Adult female moths assist with procreation by gathering pollen from one flower, rolling it into a ball, flying to another flower, and stuffing the package into the stigma before depositing their eggs in the yucca's ovaries. The moth's larvae feed on fruits and seeds, always leaving some to ripen. Thus two of life's cycles continue.

Fall Aspens

MORE THAN JUST pallid cousins of eastern species that blush during Indian summers, autumnal aspens endow the mountains of southeastern Utah with glory. They add grace notes of yellow and white to the symphony of cerulean sky and red rocks and green ponderosas. Their trunks sway in fall breezes, straight-limbed and supple, waltzing to inaudible tunes. While leaf whisperings spread balm on the sun-blasted soul, their shadows dapple the forest floor.

The trembling relative of poplars and cottonwoods, *Populus tremuloides* impresses with superlatives. As the most widespread deciduous tree in this region, it also occupies the greatest range of any tree in North America. The eponymous leaf wagging of "quakies" lets light filter through to lower branches. Aspen bark, which is often tinged green, contains additional chlorophyll, boosting photosynthesis and thus growth before the long letting-go of winter.

Elk feed on the inner bark and leaves; black bears scar the papery outer layer as they climb aspens or claw them out of sheer exuberance. The wood burns hot and with little smoke. After a tree dies, the center decays, which eases the hollowing-out of its trunk. This makes dead log sections desired material for Native American drums.

At about eight thousand feet—above the piñon-juniper and scrub oak belts and wherever water is abundant—groves of cold-resistant aspen cling to hollows or clutter entire mountainsides. They prefer to colonize burnt areas, letting a lush understory spring up in their shade, sheltering an ecosystem of great diversity. What looks like a forest of individual trees is in fact a mosaic of genetically identical sprouts from separate, horizontal taproot systems. The simultaneous turning of leaves right after frost stills these ranges yields aboveground proof for the existence of long-lived super-organisms. While single trees can survive for 150 years, clone colonies may date back to the last episode of Pleistocene glaciations. As a member of a species that thrives on mobility, I envy these trees their longstanding memories of just one place.

ANIMALS

Far off in the early evening haze I notice a column of about fifty specks spinning around an invisible hub like some oddball mobile. Gray undersides of two-toned wings shimmer in the fading light.

Coyote

BELOW A DROP-OFF, canine tracks intercept the zippered prints of chipmunk feet in the wash. Coyotes left them, trailing their main prey at this time of year. Last night I lay awake for hours, listening to yips and howls issuing from the moon-bleached mesa, to deranged laughter flying back and forth. Coyotes mate for life and travel hundreds of miles searching for food or to establish territories. Wildlife biologists believe the voice of *Canis latrans*—the "barking dog"—broadcasts the location of individuals and reunites mated pairs before and after a hunt.

Around noon I surprise the tan shape of the animal slinking downcanyon. According to the Diné, "the dark rain clouds are on his body, as is the yellow light of breaking day and evening twilight." A pale coat absorbs less heat than darker pelts and provides camouflage against a backdrop of sand and canyon walls. Hair that is shorter and thinner than the fur of other canines sheds excess heat; the animal's pared-down size (half that of wolves) helps to minimize food and water requirements.

Diné mythology abounds with stories of Coyote playing tricks on people, other animals, and even the Holy Beings. These tales can only be spun between first frost and last thaw. One recounts how Ma'ii, or Slim Trotter, was created when sky and earth briefly touched a long time ago. Another explains the black tip of his tail: when Ma'ii stole fire from the gods they chased him with lightning bolts, singeing his rear appendage. Coyote is without scruples, a buffoon and creator, a flawed hero without whom the world would not exist in its present form.

When I whistle at the smoke-like trickster he stops, turns, gives me a weary look, then continues his search for fat rodents and other delicious morsels. He has good reason to be suspicious of humans. Some people gas and burn pups in their dens. They shoot coyotes on sight, catch them with leg-hold irons or wire snares. They poison bait, or hide cyanide-firing traps in carrion. Despite these efforts, in many places "song dogs" are more numerous today than they were in pre-Columbian times.

Turkey Vultures

EVERYBODY IS FAMILIAR with the somber shapes of cartoon characters that—hunkered on Saguaro cacti—scrutinize a thirsting man's death. Sometimes mistaken for buzzards (but closely related to storks), turkey vultures perform an important function in Southwestern ecosystems. They dispose of carcasses and recycle nutrients, and the maligned species' scientific name *Cathartes aura* appropriately translates as "golden cleanser." Yet even some wildlife lovers detest nature's undertakers for their baldness, their crude table manners, and their octogenarians' necks.

Far off in the early evening haze I notice a column of about fifty specks spinning around an invisible hub like some oddball mobile. Individual parts change position, spiraling in a gravity-defying dance without ever colliding. Gray undersides of two-toned wings shimmer in the fading light. Ornithologists, who normally shun lyricisms, refer to these masses of swirling, roiling, seething vultures as "kettles." Heeding an imperceptible clue, birds suddenly start to break away from the top of the thermal updraft, streaming northward in a broad band. Wings locked and flapping only occasionally, they surge toward the magenta horizon as if drawn by magnetic fields.

I have just witnessed part of the annual spring migration of turkey vultures—next to condors America's largest birds of prey—in their return from wintering grounds in Mexico. Venues (not "flocks") of vultures commute above the land, sailing from thermal to thermal, conserving energy in the process. They use the same strategy to scan the desert floor for dead or dying animals. Unlike most birds, they possess a keen sense of smell to locate their food. On six-foot wings, vultures cruise at very low speeds without sacrificing maneuverability, by diminishing turbulence with fanned primary feathers. Poised to coast downward and forward, they miraculously continue to ascend, because the warm air that lifts them rises faster than they fall. Every hang glider pilot is familiar with the principle.

Former Arches park ranger and renegade writer Edward Abbey wanted to be reincarnated as one of these "windhovers." To me vultures are necessary and elegant and mysterious—silent messengers carrying another summer on their iridescent backs.

Beaver

THE NEW DAY BREAKS over a river layered with golden mist. After launching my canoe I sneak by a beaver on shore that is too busy to notice me. In the profound silence to which I have become accustomed I hear it gnaw on a willow branch. Slick fur glistens darkly in the sun, insulating a body, which the current itself streamlined over millennia. I look in vain for a lodge or a dam. Wider, more voluminous streams like the Colorado or Green defy the animal's engineering skills, and beavers forego construction projects altogether. They simply inhabit burrows in the riverbanks where canoeists can sometimes surprise them at low water. Winters with little snow free *Castor canadensis* from the need to cache food stores of branches and bark under the ice near lodges; instead, desert beavers come to shore for snacks whenever they want.

Beavers that *do* lay wickerwork dams across smaller perennial streams perform valuable services: They create wetland habitats for many other species. The resulting marshes also act as sponges, trapping topsoil and sediment, curtailing flash flooding and arroyo cutting.

The brown gold of plews lured some of the earliest explorers into Utah's backwaters during the 1820s and 1830s. One such trapper-adventurer—Denis Julien from St. Louis—traveled by boat, leaving inscriptions in Cataract and Labyrinth canyons. William Wolfskill trapped the San Juan River in 1822; Jedediah Smith hunted near present-day Zion four years later. The fur boom contributed much to the mapping, opening, and commercialization of territories still largely controlled by Mexico. During the heyday of the skin business about 100,000 beaver pelts per year were converted into gentlemen's top hats. This industry pushed North America's largest rodent to the brink of extinction. Luckily around 1850 the European craze for headgear made from the luscious fur shifted to fashions of Chinese silk. The animal that altered Southwestern landscapes long before humans built roads, dams, and power lines just barely escaped the fate of the passenger pigeon or Carolina parakeet.

Common Ravens

SPYING ME in my canyon hideout, a pair of ravens swoops down to investigate, rejoicing hoarsely, their plumage glossy, like Japanese lacquer boxes. The winged shadows are welcome companions on my desert wanderings. At times they follow me for hours, as faithful as black labs hoping to be fed scraps from my meals. I once left a backpack unattended only to find upon my return that ravens were pulling a sock from a newly pecked hole.

Ravens are intelligent scavengers, vocal and highly social animals, and their level of problem-solving has been compared with that of canines. In the Grand Canyon they have learned to make a living by raiding recreational boaters. Camps left unguarded are shamelessly ransacked for granola and cheese, for crackers and jerky. The ubiquitous birds get most of their water and nutriment from carrion, rodents, birds' eggs, and insects. Together with vultures they can often be seen near lion kills, black-frocked waiters eager to see the last guest leave. Ravens bond for life, and breeding pairs establish nests buffered by widely spaced territories. Less fortunate juveniles gang up nightly to brawl in communal roosts.

Raven claims a place in Native American myth next to Coyote, that other Southwestern trickster. Like *Homo sapiens*, the bird occupies a middle position between herbivore and carnivore—a two-faced creature, neither fish nor flesh, neither good nor evil. Ethnographers recorded this Southern Paiute tale: "One time Coyote and all the birds were having a meeting in a cave. Coyote was the leader and started a big fire so they could all keep warm. He was using pitch wood, which makes a lot of black smoke. Raven, being the farthest back in the cave, absorbed most of it, and that is why he is black from head to foot." The world's largest perching bird can indeed tolerate intense temperatures despite 25 percent more heat absorption through its sooty feathers (compared with lighter colored birds). Its stocky build does not favor quick heat gain or loss.

Aside from the occasional pilfering of provisions, I enjoy these clown birds and see nothing common about them. When the duo takes off with a final "quork," I feel strangely abandoned.

Desert Bears

THE STATUS of desert bears has been precarious ever since the first wagons arrived here. A tightfisted environment curbs their numbers and compels the largest land-borne flesh eaters to be quite eclectic in their appetites. Despite this limitation grizzlies are thought to have been rather common in the piñon-juniper woodlands of the Southwest until around 1850. Ranchers, sheepherders, and government trappers considered them a threat to livestock and people's sense of superiority. They waged a lengthy war of extermination that ended in 1979 with the killing of a lone sow in Colorado's San Juan Mountains. Although unsubstantiated sightings have been reported, that female was probably the last individual of a branch of *Ursus arctos horribilis*, which is now considered regionally extinct. The grizzly's wild and free presence still graces the flag of California, one of the states comprising its former hunting grounds.

Black bears have fared slightly better than their more demanding and conspicuous cousins. Like shadows and largely unmolested they roam the Abajo and La Sal mountains, as well as the Tavaputs Plateau of southeastern Utah. They also survive in more southerly pockets on "sky islands," forested ranges thrust above the Arizona desert. But these subpopulations suffer from isolation and inbreeding. Although they are born wanderers, very few dare to cross belts of saltbush and sage to vitalize adjoining enclaves. Genetically homogenous groups become susceptible to changes in the environment. When bear populations reach their critical size, another keystone species drops out of already impoverished habitats. At this point biologists argue about the numbers required to keep different species healthy and from getting sucked into the maelstrom of extinction.

We need large predators in our wilderness like we need clean air to breathe. They grease the gears of ecosystems by keeping a check on rodents and deer, by weeding out the old and unfit from the gene pool. In addition, bears satisfy a craving for connection that lies deeply enfolded within human existence. In their presence our pulse quickens, our senses rejuvenate.

Great Horned Owl

CAMPED IN a nameless canyon, I witness a strange encounter. On the verge of sunset a great horned owl attacks a raven in the boulders close by. The fight is orchestrated with much wing flapping and sinister beak clapping.

The big owl *does* have a dubious reputation with Anglos, Diné, Paiutes, and even Romans of classical antiquity. Its Latin name (*Bubo virginianus*) stresses the link with death by associating the bird with the plague that all but depopulated medieval Europe. Paiute Indians kept diminutive burrowing owls as pets but did not use the feathers of their larger relatives, because they considered great horned owls harbingers of bad luck. Mexican witches are said to shape-shift into owls. For Pueblo Indians like the Hopi, plumes from the silent prowlers tied to bags of human excrement are among the vilest implements of sorcery.

Owls occasionally nest in abandoned cliff dwellings, which many Diné avoid for fear of provoking the spirits of ancestral enemies. Other traits that may make the masked birds suspicious or even loathsome are their mesmerizing amber eyes, soundless flight, and their "horns," which really are feather tufts. In its monotony their hooting recalls the forlornness of condemned souls. Preying on ravens, smaller owls, and hawks up to the size of redtails is behavior deemed cannibalistic by humans who routinely exterminate millions of their own kind in systematic campaigns.

A mythological reason for the condemnation of this recluse may be found in a Diné creation story. At present-day Shiprock, New Mexico, Monster Slayer killed a giant bird that tried to feed him to its young. After that the mythical hero turned to the orphaned nestlings. He swung the older around by the legs—four times—ordaining that it should furnish bones and plumes for the People. The bird flapped away as an eagle. He swung the younger around and told it that men would listen to its voice to learn of the future; and what greater threat could be envisioned? That bird left the roost as an owl.

Mountain Lion

"MICHAEL!" "WHAT?" "LION!" I peel from my sleeping bag, eyes crusty with sleep. My hiking companion excitedly motions for me to come to where she bedded down in the slickrock gully. "Where?" I whisper, unaware that I'm not even wearing pants. But she has lost sight of the big cat that froze upon hearing us. It now blends in with the sandstone, a superb example of predator camouflage.

You may not see a mountain lion in the wild in a lifetime. But they are out there, watching from behind boulders and pines. The cat, which the Diné call "one who walks stealthily behind rocks," largely sticks to isolated mesas, preferring areas humans seldom visit. It has good reasons to be wary of people. Trophy hunters, ranchers, and trappers of the federal Animal Damage Control Program have decimated mountain lions for decades, upsetting the balance of predator-prey relationships. *Felis concolor* supposedly depletes deer populations and wreaks havoc on sheep and cattle, and many Western states classify it as a varmint. Other labels for the sleek, solitary stalker include puma, cougar, catamount, panther, and polecat—for its tendency to climb trees when cornered by hunting dogs.

Mountain lions inhabit the continent from Argentina to Canada, and at one time patrolled all 48 states of the continental U.S. Their population is still relatively strong in the Southwest, estimated at 3,000 animals. Male adult lions can be nine feet from the tip of their tail to their whiskers and weigh as much as a sturdy person. Despite their size they are nimble hunters, leaping 20 to 30 feet and outrunning mule deer at short distances. In times of scarcity, mountain lions feed on porcupines, rabbits, feral burros, mice, birds, and the occasional sheep or cow. Even careless joggers have become prey.

The lion finally moves again, rippling over rock benches like water, a buff embodiment of power and grace. At the canyon rim it pauses briefly. Its profile against the desert sky stays forever etched in my memory.

Black Widow

HANGING MOTIONLESS UPSIDE-DOWN in her silk funnel, a black widow guards the entrance to a pre-Columbian granary. The red hourglass—in stark contrast to her inky abdomen—strikes me as the perfect symbol for a culture that ran out of time.

The black widow is one of the truly detested and feared creatures of the greater Southwest, producing some of the most lethal venom known to humankind. Native Americans used the crushed bodies of these spiders for arrowhead poison in an early version of chemical warfare. The bloated-looking spider with the scarlet stop sign is actually rather timid and withdraws when disturbed outside her nest. She places her silk tube at the base of the catch web, often hidden in rock crevices or in the walls of old buildings. The web can be several feet wide and is spun from the strongest silk of any spider around; it ensnares thousands of insects per year in a sticky embrace.

Males of the species, which are much smaller, are light brown and nonvenomous. One puny suitor almost always hangs out on the fringes of a widow's lair, infatuated and flirting with disaster. Unjustly singled out from other arachnids as a voracious man-eater, the widow mates only once in her lifetime, retaining some of the sperm for future egg laying. She carefully wraps a batch of between 3,000 and 5,000 eggs in a protective silk sack, which she then hangs near the web. The normally shy spider turns aggressive when defending her cream-colored egg cocoon. Motherly instinct does not only grow on the mammalian branch of life's tree.

Explosions of spider populations occur during rainy summers, but hatchlings disperse soon and are rarely seen until maturity. Although immature females are at first brightly splotched (as shown in the photo), most develop an orange-white hourglass that darkens with age. Widows crawl about suddenly in the spring, at the end of hibernation. And when the inconspicuous youngsters mature later in the year—becoming more obvious—there seems to be a sudden outbreak of black widows.

Desert Bighorn Sheep

I DROP MY PACK in a stand of ravaged Gambel's oaks whose tops have been clipped by strong winds charging down the gorge. A petroglyph panel has hooked my attention, knee-high above ground and half-hidden by sagebrush. It depicts two styles of bighorn sheep—round bellied, with dots, and box-shaped, with bands—the latter perhaps mimicking split willow figurines excavated from caves. Archaic hunters at home in this out-of-the-way place left traces that challenge our imagination.

Desert bighorn sheep are the most common images in Southwestern rock art; their importance for prehistoric peoples equals that of cattle for open-range ranchers. Sheep were not only an important source of meat for the local Fremont Indians who killed them in cliff drives or cornered them on narrow ledges to stone them to death. They were also valued for their hides and horns, which yielded clothing and tools. Overhunting by trophy-seekers in combination with introduced diseases and competition from domestic sheep and goats decimated bighorn numbers around the end of the nineteenth century. Wild sheep were reintroduced after the 1920s where they had become extinct.

Both sexes grow horns, but those of ewes only amount to short, curvy spikes. Rams, however, sprout impressive curls. Measuring thirty inches from tips to bases, these appendages seem grotesquely out of proportion to their bodies. Record spirals take about eight years to fully develop. Head-butting contests can last for hours and help establish a mating hierarchy among males. Pool table sounds glance off canyon walls during the fall rut, and the clacking of skulls led Diné hunters to believe that thunder originates with the battering rams.

As true desert denizens, bighorn sheep are well adapted to drought conditions and capable of tolerating extreme dehydration—up to 20 percent loss of body weight. They usually metabolize water from moist grasses and shrubs that make up their diet but need to drink at waterholes during dry spells. There the sure-footed rock climbers become vulnerable to predation from mountain lions or to human cunning.

Rufous Hummingbird

THE ABILITIES OF HUMMINGBIRDS never cease to amaze me. Spring and summer residents in these canyons, they travel to winter in Mexico from as far north as Alaska—no mean feat for birds the size of a finger.

They achieve the maximum speed of a bicyclist (over thirty miles an hour), beating their wings up to eighty times per second, according to species. Each kind therefore produces a characteristic whir, by which—theoretically at least—it can be identified. Flight muscles in this little athlete amount to one-third of its total body weight, enabling it to fly backward and sideways in lofty dueling and delectable feeding routines on nectar-filled flower tubes. It is the only bird capable of doing so.

Hummingbirds have the highest metabolic rate of any warm-blooded creature and sip voraciously to keep the engine stoked—except for breeding females. To conserve energy they lapse into torpor at night and during cool days, lowering body temperature by fifty degrees, cutting their caloric needs by two-thirds.

Unlike color-blind insects attracted by smell, hummingbirds locate their meals by sight and are particularly fond of bright-red blossoms. On one occasion a hummer briefly mistook the crimson stripes of socks, which I had hung out to dry, for a source of nourishment.

Another time I watched a rufous hummingbird assault a sparrow hawk, reversing their usual roles. The runt was bullying a target three times his size. Like a dive-bomber he circled around, again and again, to renew his charge from above. I am sure it was a male, because the breeding season was over, and females would already be incubating. A hen's strategy is to avoid predation by camouflage. Freezing on her thimble of a nest, a female will mantle two pea-sized eggs. Males on the other hand are aggressive; they often defend hummingbird feeders against several rivals at once. In the end boldness won the day, and much to my delight the little guy succeeded in driving away the hawk.

PEOPLE

In their complementary view of the universe,
the Diné perceive gentle spring rains as female,
bearing fertility, tickling crops into sprouting.

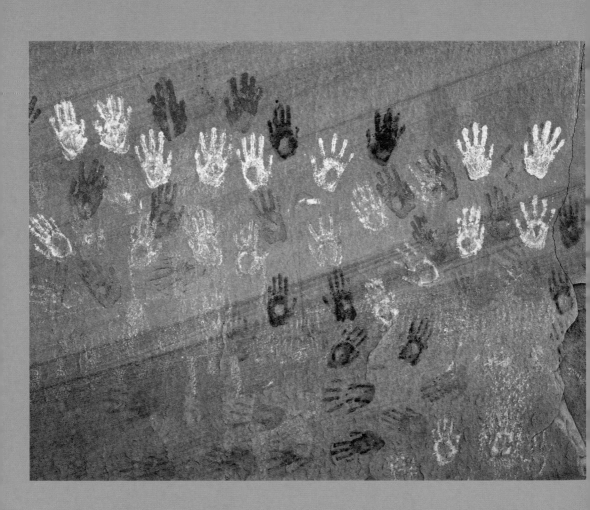

Ancient Symbols

A PICTOGRAPH PANEL with symbols by the Hopi Indians' Basketmaker ancestors emblazons an undercut at Natural Bridges National Monument. Lines wiggling across the rock face possibly document the migration routes of family groups to new homelands. They could be maps of these rambling creeks, or else snakes, which were associated with fertility and water. Their popularity in rock art comes as no surprise; the scaly forms of serpents and their way of propulsion evoke this country's reptilian physique. Most of these images lack the sophistication of the Barrier Canyon style of earlier Desert Archaic hunter-gatherers. And yet, one sticks out from the rest—a figure eight, drawn in white and lying on its side. In mathematics it signifies infinity. I ponder it like a spell in an unfamiliar language.

Perhaps for those who walked here before, it symbolized rebirth, the cyclical bending of time. The crux of this figure lies of course where both loops cross: the sacred center, braced by the four cardinal directions. Choose one direction, any one, on the eight and you will return to the world's navel, to start again. *That* is true immortality.

On Cedar Mesa another panel surprises with a smattering of handprints, which spread disembodied across a billboard-sized sandstone facade. This register has been stamped with hematite contained in the red mud of a nearby seep. "We lived here first!" it declares. Children's handprints mingle with those of adults. Some look corrugated, an effect achieved by striating one hand with mud applied by the fingertips of the other. I imagine that—rather than claiming territory—people tried to absorb the land through their palms, using wet clay as a conductor. Avoiding the prints, I press my left hand against the wall's sandpaper texture and sense a current running along my heart line. I feel connected by this simple act, learning more about the canyon's inhabitants than from stacks of books. But I do not deceive myself. Ultimately they remain foreign to me, as foreign as their art.

Diné

THE DINÉ ARE FAMOUS for hand-woven butterfly blankets and silver-and-turquoise jewelry that rivals the gaudiness of desert skies. The tribe has about 270,000 members, representing the second-most numerous North American Indian group. (Only the Cherokee outnumber it.) Most Diné live on a reservation half the size of New England, largest in the nation. Closely related to Apaches and the Northern Athabaskans of western Canada and interior Alaska, they arrived relatively late in the Southwest. As part of a second wave, nomadic bands swept into the New World via the Bering land bridge in search of mammoth and other Pleistocene megafauna. Sometime between A.D. 1300 and A.D. 1500 they "settled" near the upper Rio Grande.

Yielding to Hispanic and Anglo-American pressure the Diné turned to pastoralism. Introduced sheep became an important source of wool, meat, and cultural identity during the reservation era. The name *Navajo* possibly originated with the Tewa, a Puebloan people in New Mexico. Navahuu were the "enemies of the cultivated fields." This epithet harkens back to a time when raiding sedentary neighbors (as well as marrying them or trading with them) was a way of life in a demanding place. We know many Native American tribes only through outsiders' derogatory words. Because of the negative connotations the Navajos' own term, *Diné*—people—is preferable.

Hexagonal structures of mud-chinked, peeled logs are the unmistakable Diné homesteads. Domes of red earth crown some older, five-sided hogans, which mesh perfectly with their surroundings. The dried mud skin provides insulation. Like saguaro cacti for the Sonoran Desert, the Diné's mounded habitations have become icons for the Colorado Plateau. As in many anthills, their entrances face eastward to welcome each new sun and its warmth on brisk winter mornings. Although the newer, horizontal log-style dwelling only evolved after 1900, it encapsulates cosmological references that were handed down from generation to generation. Individual architectural elements like roof beams or corner posts, but also the building as a whole, represent features of the Diné universe. Where the world was home, the home became world.

Kiva

CRUISING UP THE TRAIL as if on autopilot, I almost miss the archaeological gem I plan to revisit. A random glance from the tips of my boots to the rock shelves above snags on wood beams too easily mistaken for dead junipers. A short scramble brings me to mud-daubed granaries. Wedged into the depths of an overhang, they lie cradled against sun and rain. A reconstructed ladder disappears into the ground. Gingerly, I step down its rungs into a kiva that feels freshly abandoned.

Contemporary Puebloans like the Hopi gather in similar chambers during annual rites, to maintain equilibrium in the world. Convoluted prayers and rituals plead with the spirits, propagating the rains needed for growing crops. Only adult male clan members convene underground to perform the secret parts of ceremonies.

Saffron-colored light swarming with dust motes slants through the kiva's entrance hatch. As my eyes adjust, I am able to discern details. Plaster coats walls of rough-hewn sandstone, and where it has crumbled the underlying mortar reveals centuries-old fingerprints. Four niches now occupied by packrats once held religious paraphernalia. The bottom half of the wall shows the original pink clay slip. Soot blackens the upper half, demarcating light and dark with a crisp line. Could this be a representation of the red earth and the night sky above?

Details of Pueblo sacral architecture are known to hold cosmic significance. This kiva's flagstone-lined entrance, for example, is aligned due south. Blue-gray circles on the inside wall face east and west. (Standing in for sun and moon, perhaps?) The fire pit takes center stage; an upright stone slab sheltered flames against drafts from a vent in the wall. North of the fire pit the Sípapu opens, a fist-sized hole in the floor. Hopi myths recall how people emerged from it into this fourth world, after the Holy Beings destroyed previous planes of existence to punish humans for sloth and greed.

Touched by a breath of the sacred I leave stone mortars, dry corncobs, and corrugated pottery shards to their stillness.

Pilgrims

IN OUR SECULAR SOCIETY rites of passage have largely fallen by the wayside. Baptisms, weddings, and funerals still generate some meaning. But for adolescents, acts unrelated to the mysteries of existence—high school graduation or getting a driver's license, for example—normally signify the transition into adulthood.

The Hopi of northeastern Arizona's Third Mesa followed a time-honored custom of initiating young men into tribal realities by sending them on a quest fraught with uncertainty and danger. The gathering of sacred salt from natural deposits deep in the Grand Canyon was the obvious motive; but personal transformation lay at the heart of this mission. Upon their successful return from the chasm salt pilgrims were initiated into the Wúwuchim, a men's society.

Two cairns at the edge of a tributary canyon pinpoint the path that unwinds into this netherworld, which is also considered the domain of the dead. Before pilgrims set out they offered pinches of cornmeal to the four directions. If asked with pure heart, Tawa the sun god would grant good weather and a safe journey.

A few miles from the salt crystallizing on the Colorado River's banks, a huge yellowish mound swells from the underbrush like an earthen breast. This is the Sípapu, one of the holiest places of the Four Corners. The fifty-foot-wide travertine dome enshrines a spring that many Hopi associate with the umbilical cord. Through a hole in the top people first emerged into this world—an event reenacted each time a masked Kachina dancer climbs from a kiva during ceremonies on Third Mesa. Echoing creation stories from our own tradition, human ancestors had incited divine wrath with their arrogance and depravity. At length the gods destroyed three consecutive realms, enlisting fire and flood. A few people escaped the most recent deluge, assisted by Spider Woman who provided a reed that served as a ladder. Our present home is also the last. Hopi elders stress the need to take good care of it. Like them we have roots as pilgrims in a New World.

Mavericks

HIS REAL NAME was George Leroy Parker. He died in a shootout with federal troops in a cow town in southern Bolivia in 1907. Thus ended a career of bank and train robberies that ran like a string from Canada to the Mexican border, into Peru, Argentina, Bolivia. The world knew him as Butch Cassidy, leader of the Wild Bunch, partner of the equally disreputable Harry Longabaugh (a.k.a. the Sundance Kid) who shared his fate, spilling blood in the same dusty courtyard of a San Vicente inn. According to one theory, Cassidy survived and returned to the United States where he lived quietly until 1937 under an assumed name. In a similar vein Everett Ruess— a footloose, romantic artist from California—in 1934 supposedly staged his own disappearance in the Escalante watershed to settle anonymously with a Diné wife on the reservation. Some people speculate that the youth chanced upon cattle rustlers in Davis Gulch who murdered him and then hid the body. Apparently, our sensibilities will not condone violent ends for Western folk heroes. Weaned on Hollywood fare, we need them to ride the range forever.

Robbers Roost was only one of many hideouts of the Wild Bunch and other, lesser known bandits, a redrock citadel engulfed by the most remote quarter of the continental United States. Similar refuges for gangs were located in the forested folds of the Henry Mountains and along the infamous Outlaw Trail that linked Wyoming with New Mexico. A showdown took place in Robbers Roost in 1899 between the Moab sheriff, backed by a posse, and the horse thieves Silver Tip, Blue John, and "half-breed" Ed Newcomb. After some desultory gunplay the outlaws escaped, but the law's long reach had finally found the Roost.

Rock inscriptions in the Burr Desert's badlands remind us of turbulent days in southeastern Utah. These often fanciful cowboy-glyphs are now considered antiquities—American heirlooms on par with pre-Columbian ruins and pictographs. They are under federal protection, and defacing them would make you an outlaw yourself.

Cliff Dwellings

FROM THE TRAIL I scan rust-red splotches along a gallery traversing the cliffs up high. They look too symmetrical to be natural. So—through the musk of serviceberry blossoms—I climb two hundred feet to a gaping mouth stuffed with ruins and pictographs invisible from below. Rock slabs seal the hatches in wattle-and-daub granaries, securing their contents against mice and other looters. A flagstone circle outlines the roof of a subterranean ceremonial chamber on the alcove's floor. Aware of how rickety this structure is, I decide not to enter. A perimeter wall resembling breastworks rings the kiva and its secondary buildings. Portholes flank the approach, suitable for showering arrows and stones on attackers. While I study the debris of people long dead I wonder what drove them to live like eagles in forbidding roosts.

About 800 years ago inhabitants of the Southwest commonly known as Anasazi (but more correctly labeled ancestral Puebloans) began constructing redoubts like Hovenweep Castle on a mesa near the present-day state line between Utah and Colorado. Their predecessors had long felt safe in pit houses or in large pueblos without fortifications. Strongholds at Mesa Verde, Cedar Mesa, and Navajo National Monument, as well as pictographs of spear-wielding warriors, and grisly archaeological finds indicate that around A.D. 1200 times were indeed tough. South-facing alcoves give shade in the summer and reflect warmth from a low-angle winter sun; they also shelter cliff dwellers from cutting winds. But these advantages are not enough to explain the move into habitations that were difficult to build and easy to defend. Piecing together the puzzle, archaeologists concluded that late-period ancestral Puebloans suffered chronic raiding and possibly internal strife. Environmental degradation and climate change had initiated their demise.

Two lizards doing push-ups on a sandstone sill divert my attention. They benefit from the same southern exposure that attracted the Ancient Ones to this site. Tread lightly, the ruins caution us. Eventually they will turn to dust. Outlasting them, the sun will warm rocks for generations of lizards to come.

Archaeo-Astronomy

ON THIS LONGEST DAY of the year the sun arcs across unblemished blue before the northern hemisphere swings back on its winter trajectory. Light knifes through a keyhole slit and across the Entrada Sandstone, where it forms a radiant dagger. Within seconds the beam mutates into an arrowhead—razor-edged, notched, and tapering to a perfect point—that aims downward, at the head of a snake petroglyph. Skillfully rendered, the body flexes for more than thirty feet. Six dips and seven crests scroll into the shape of a 900-year-old reptile, adding up to the total of new moons in a year. The light show lasts about half a minute before the bright star hurries on.

Our need to perceive order in a universe baffling in its complexity and unpredictability led us to become diligent sky gazers. Ancient civilizations not only personified celestial bodies; they elevated them to the status of gods whose pacing governs human lives. In Mesopotamia, India, Meso-America, and Bronze-Age Europe, astronomer-priests evolved, specialists who monitored and appeased these deities. Their observations provided dates for rituals, feasts, or pilgrimages, as well as practical advice for the planting and harvesting of crops.

Sedentary agriculturalists like the Hopi and their predecessors determined the time of year by means of horizon calendars. Topographic quirks in the skyline or built towers helped them to calibrate sunrises and sunsets for different seasons. Around solstices the sun's horizontal drift slows, and it practically rises in the same place for a week. For historic Pueblo dwellers winter solstice in particular was a time of existential dread; they feared that the land, or life itself, might grind to a halt, seized with unending cold. Elaborate festivals were therefore held to send the sun on its way again.

A stone chamber at Hovenweep Castle is commonly known as the Sun Room. During solstice sunsets—winter and summer—light seeps through different portholes, illuminating the lintels of opposing doorways. The spots' daily progress enabled observers to forecast the sun's inertia and gave people time to arrange the required festivities.

Great Gallery

AN APPENDIX OF Canyonlands National Park boasts one of the greatest treasures of the Colorado Plateau: the Great Gallery. This pictograph panel has become the standard for Barrier Canyon rock inscriptions, a style named for the streamlet that splashes through Horseshoe Canyon.

From afar I glimpse a procession of mummy shapes marching across a cliff band. About twenty-five life-size figures, plus what seem to be children, jostle on a frieze more than 100 feet long. Some are clad in festive attire—adorned with what I take to be fringes, beads, or shells—and accompanied by a few animals of indistinct nature. One figure is carrying "twins." A specter with empty eye sockets is usually interpreted as a powerful shaman, guardian spirit, or Herculean ancestor. Barrier Canyon rock art lacks weaponry of any kind; this absence has been related to functional differences. Rather than involving hunting magic, these scenes might reenact tribal myths. The panel makers mixed paint from crushed iron oxide and applied it directly with their fingers or with yucca fiber brushes, or else indirectly, by blowing pigment through reed tubes. Then they engraved lines into it for additional texture and depth.

Members of the Desert Archaic culture whose earliest arrival in this area has been dated to 7,000 years ago explored feeder canyons of the Colorado and Green rivers. Staying there for at least part of the year, they snared rabbits and birds, collected seeds, roots, and berries, drawing sustenance from a desert. Unlike the agricultural Puebloans, who succeeded them on adjacent lands but much later, these footloose women and men did not bother with pottery or adobe. They only left their visionary art and a few arrowheads.

Looking at these expressions of obsolete lifeways, it is hard not to project modern sensibilities and attitudes onto smooth stone. Even our interpretation of them as "art" is inappropriate, compartmentalizing existence. I try to keep my brain from spoiling the magic and instead share the artists' humanity across an abyss of time.

Flute Player

THE SPACIOUS INTERSECTION of two canyons has attracted human attention for a long time. Hogan beams silvered with age are the most recent signs of occupation. A rock art panel on a south-facing alcove wall predates them by far. Its Miro-style stick figures have not been vandalized, which—given their proximity to Lake Powell's reservoir—comes as a surprise.

The image of most interest to me here is a flute player that has begun to melt into underlying sandstone. Commonly mistaken for Kokopelli, it depicts the Hopi Flute Clan deity or its helper Maahu, the cicada. Ancestors of the Hopi most likely painted this image to document the clan's passage toward its current home in Arizona.

After their emergence into the Fourth World, people split up and followed separate routes to lands the creator had chosen for them. Traveling to each of the four directions, to where land meets the sea, they claimed this new world. Although they stopped frequently and built villages along the way, they would in time abandon those and return to settle in a promised land, a land that was to be theirs forever. In the course of their wanderings, the people branched again and again, forming the clans, which organize present-day Hopi society. Each clan treasures stories—and symbols like the flute player   that are relevant to these sojourns. The Hopi also commemorate clan migrations during annual festivals and reenact them in pilgrimages.

Archaeologists support Hopi assertions of kinship with cliff dwellers at Canyon de Chelly, Keet Seel, and Betatakin. Some ancestral Puebloans left their drought-ridden fields and settlements to live on one of three Hopi mesas. Others moved to the upper Rio Grande Valley, founding mud-plastered pueblos snug and busy as cliff swallow colonies.

In the case of much extant rock art the bottle remains, while the message was lost. Yet the appeal of symbols prevails, powerful even after specific meanings have dissolved. To me, the flute player is a pied piper whose tune pulls me forever into these canyons. His instrument unlocks portals to some of our last refuges.

Warriors

BETWEEN UTAH'S ABAJO MOUNTAINS and the Colorado River's vast trench stretches a world of Cedar Mesa sandstone, a land of buttes, pinnacles, grottoes, domes, and hoodoos known as The Needles. This district of Canyonlands National Park holds vestiges of a pre-Columbian past that equal the archaeological riches of adjoining Cedar Mesa. Its canyons promise not only relief from the desert's glare, but also countless surprises: ancestral Puebloan ruins and Fremont rock art panels; a plethora of natural arches; two different ecosystems; perennial springs; and the skeletons of nineteenth-century ranches.

Before the trail climbs for a shortcut through cleft sandstone to avoid the sandy arroyo, it skirts a park-like pocket. Twenty feet above ground, erosion has sapped the cliff. The breach frames an image only surpassed by the paintings of Horseshoe Canyon's Great Gallery. Looking through my binoculars at the crack that ascends to the opening's floor I notice how callused hands and feet of bottomland farmers have burnished the rock. From the shade of a fortified dwelling, some critter scuttles deeper into the alcove. A life-size warrior in red, white, and blue, looms above me like a twilight guardian. Archaeologists radiocarbon-dated an exfoliated charcoal flake from the site, estimating this warrior to be 750 years old. "Shield bearers" can be found throughout the area, and circular designs associated with cliff dwellings could depict clan symbols. They hint at the martial aspect of canyon domesticity, at residents whose final decline may have been accelerated by civil war or invasion.

While the temptation to locate and enter frail ruins, to touch rock art, or even to take souvenirs may be strong, we should resist it. Stone walls cave in easily; oils in the skin of our fingers destroy the delicate pigments of pictographs; and off trails, bootsteps crush biological soil crusts—black spreads of algae, bacteria, and lichens that crimp the flats, preventing erosion and converting important nutrients for plants. As in any museum, our enjoyment of exhibits should not deprive others of the pleasure of finding them intact.

PLACES

Pueblo Bonito. Bisti Badlands. Shiprock.
Rainbow Bridge. Kayenta. Cortez. Panguitch....
Spoken like mantras and in different tongues,
sonorous names conjure the land's bastard heritage.

Waterpocket Fold

TIRES ARE SPINNING, WHINING. They spew mud and rocks and start to smoke. Smelling rubber, I tell Steve to step off the gas. We are stuck up to the axles, bogged down in the middle of nowhere. I am sure if I climbed on top of the van, I could see the world's edge from there. We arrived by way of Capitol Reef's Burr Trail—an old route for cattle drives to the Colorado River—which had been partly paved over in 1986.

Where the dirt road zigzags over the Waterpocket Fold it reveals a textbook display of earth history. Usually stacked neatly like a deck of cards, sedimentary strata have dropped and now all lean at the same crazy angle, throwing up a dragon-back barrier. In less than an hour you can walk through four succesive rock formations and corresponding eras: rainbow Chinle; pumpkin Wingate; lavender Kayenta; and creamy Navajo. This layer cake is not only multihued, but each tier also manifests a signature form of erosion: crumbling hills for the Chinle; vertical cracks for the Wingate; catwalks for the Kayenta; and wrinkled humps for the Navajo sandstone. There are places along this fault where up to fifteen bedding planes lie bared to the elements simultaneously.

After hours of scraping muck, of jacking up the chassis, of putting rocks and deadwood under its wheels, we finally manage to free the van and lurch onward, to Muley Twist Canyon. Old-timers joke that the canyon's bends are tight enough to torque the rump of a pack mule.

So many arches! I count eleven, including some twin spans and am perhaps even missing a few. Peekaboo Rock, which overlooks the trailhead, is a barely perforated fin, a very young arch geologically speaking. The center of an ivory-colored wall weathered and collapsed here, exposing a cobalt patch of sky. As erosion continues it will enlarge this window. Frost, water, and heat will wrench away more supportive rock, to perhaps someday free another crescent from its matrix. Compared with this youngster, Delicate Arch, whose image graces Utah's Centennial license plates, is a Methuselah ready to expire.

The Confluence

IN JULY 1869, John Wesley Powell—explorer of the Green and Colorado rivers—camped in the canyonlands' terra incognita near the meeting of waters. To scout the stretch ahead, Major Powell and one companion climbed to a promontory south of the present-day Overlook Trail in The Needles. Contemplating the scene, the otherwise stern leader and geologist waxed poetic:

"What a world of grandeur is spread before us—wherever we look there is but a wilderness of rocks; deep gorges, where the rivers are lost below cliffs and towers and pinnacles; and ten thousand strangely carved forms in every direction; and beyond them, mountains blending with the clouds."

Looking upstream, Powell surveyed the tight, sinuous twists of the Green River or Rio Verde, which his party had descended. Its source is snow falling more than 700 miles away in Wyoming's Wind River Range. From the northeast an identical chasm merges with that of the Green, overshadowed by a headland the major dubbed Junction Butte. That tributary originates in Colorado's Rocky Mountain National Park, just shy of the Continental Divide; it was formerly known as the Grand River. Spanish and Mexican explorers called the stream's lower reaches Rio Colorado or Red River, for its turbid floods. Early-nineteenth-century Anglos and Spaniards did not know that the Colorado runs 1,450 miles to the sea, forming the largest watershed in the Southwest, draining one-twelfth of the continental United States.

By the time I approach the place where two rivers kiss, my canoe has sprung a leak. Water from a hole in the keel sloshes around my sandaled feet. It is the result of plowing across too many gravel bars. I console myself with the thought that at this point Powell (one-armed, no less) had already endured worse: moldy flour, rancid bacon, storms and shipwrecks, even the loss of a boat. But he continued from here, unable to ignore the siren song of adventure. "We have an unknown distance yet to run, an unknown river to explore," reads his journal entry from the canyon's belly.

Natural Bridges

I DROP BELOW blunt sandstone rims, immediately losing sight of the parking lot, ready to escape to the privacy of Natural Bridges National Monument. At the bottom of Armstrong Canyon the effects created by last night's cold snap stir my curiosity.

Concentric air pockets collar rocks in the creek bed, vitreous as cross-sections of agate. Shell ice crunches under my boots like old bones. Frost feathers the sand, contrasting with miniature dunes of ribbed sediment. Transparent lids display cottonwood leaves at a pool's bottom: fall souvenirs locked in glass paperweights. Water ripples have solidified into sheets. On their way up, bubbles congealed into silvery dimes, arrested in mid-motion, and are kept from bursting until next spring. Time itself seems to have frozen.

Armstrong Canyon is a place where human and natural history intersect, a place claimed by many. After the cliff dwellers left, Paiute bands took possession. Their generic name for the stone bridges—Under the Horse's Belly—reflects nomadic preoccupations. In 1908, President Theodore Roosevelt set aside 7,000 acres at the head of White Canyon, to preserve three rock spans and approximately 200 archaeological sites.

Kachina Bridge is one of the monument's parabolas. Plying its 200-foot-long muscle, it outflanks a large alcove containing an ancestral Puebloan ruin and pictographs. Desert varnish veins the wall above a "false" kiva. I also find petroglyphs chiseled into the abutment, which could have provided reassurance, expressing a desire for significance in the face of nature's monumental whims. Like all natural bridges, this one owes its existence to a meandering creek. Long before people first lived on its banks it kept worrying both sides of a sandstone slab that juts like a scapula from the canyon wall. It finally shouldered its way through, gaining unhindered passage.

Farther along, Owachomo soars—old, even as natural bridges go. Shaved by the elements to a gossamer strand *only* nine feet thick, it will tumble some day. Of course, you and I might not be around when that happens; perhaps none of our kind will be. As I climb from the canyon, snow alights on my pack like down from a torn sleeping bag.

Spider Rock

A LONE FIGURE EMERGES from its molehill abode. Trailing a dog the size of a flea, it walks toward the sheep pen. I take in this bucolic scene perched on rimrock like a falcon, though admittedly with less grace. Below me unfurls Canyon de Chelly, Diné equivalent of the Trail of Tears.

The crack that spreads from the spine fastening New Mexico to Arizona provided a final stronghold in 1864, when bluecoats led by Christopher "Kit" Carson rounded up people in a scorched-earth campaign. Now the canyon is mute, except for wind sighing through dwarf junipers. Then its crags reverberated with the screaming of women and children, with the neighing of horses, with the commands of men. The troops burned cornfields and homesteads; they killed livestock; they laid waste to peach orchards and pastures. For hundreds of years the Diné had resisted pacification with all-out guerilla war. The U.S. government finally decided to remove this troublesome tribe from its homelands. Many died on the march to a hard-as-nails reservation deep in New Mexico, where Comanche raiders harassed the survivors, who lived confined and defenseless with their Apache enemies.

In the distance Spider Rock erupts from the canyon floor. Unlike other sandstone buttresses in the vicinity, the 800-foot monolith was never converted into a fortress. It is too steep to be scaled without mountaineering gear. But more importantly, nobody climbs on top of a shrine.

Spider Woman, one of the most revered deities of the Hopi and Diné pantheons, is said to dwell on this pinnacle. After she had molded humans from red clay, she attached a silk thread to each one as a reminder of obligations. She also instructed her wards in the weaving of blankets patterned in the land's pastel tones. According to tradition Spider Rock and Face Rock—a similar feature across the canyon—are petrified Holy Beings. They speak to each other in echoes that ricochet between tapestried walls.

Parents scared intractable children with stories about Spider Woman's appetites. Accounts of a bloody past were not considered bedtime fare.

Redwall Cavern

WHILE I PROP UP our folding table and start slicing watermelons the guests wander off to explore Redwall Cavern. We beached our rafts at its mouth, which gapes like a feeding whale shark's amid serried cliffs. I undo my sandals and wiggle my toes in cool, ankle-deep sand. The huge twilight cove muffles our voices.

Major Powell, who spent a night here during his first descent, thought the natural amphitheater could seat 50,000 people. One can forgive the major for overestimating the capacity of this place. Upstream, Stanton's Cave houses big-eared bats. It held 4,000-year-old artifacts, as well as the bones of Pleistocene condors and mountain goats. But unlike Stanton's, Redwall Cavern is not a true cave. Here the river simply undercut its constraining walls. Before Glen Canyon Dam was built, the Colorado periodically flooded the cavern floor, leaving not only sediment but also driftwood that warmed Powell's men.

The geologist explorer named this section Marble Canyon for its Redwall limestone, the mother rock roofing our lunch site. It is perhaps the most prominent feature in the Grand Canyon's lithic archive, a 500-foot gutter collecting the river's spillage. Solution cavities mar the canyon's flanks, dug by rainwater percolating through limestone from the plateau above. Although these hollows beg to be investigated, they are off-limits by park service decree. A shallow sea submerged much of the continent—from a mountain range in Nevada to the Appalachain foothills—during the Mississippian period about 330 to 360 million years ago. Skeletons of tiny marine organisms at its bottom melted into bedrock; many larger creatures became encased as fossils: nautiloids, corals, brachiopods, sponges, and crinoids. The term *Redwall* is really somewhat of a misnomer. Initially the scarps appear to be salmon-colored. But where chunks split off, the true blue-grey of limestone is showing. The answer to this riddle is simple. Minerals from the Hermit Shale have been staining the underlying formation.

After lunch we gather around a boulder at the cavern's entrance. Fossilized bryozoans web its glaze, lacy as ferns. We just stand there and marvel at time's fingerprints.

Dolores River

WITH 171 MILES of slickrock-and-ponderosa canyons and several class IV rapids, the Dolores River between Bradfield, Colorado, and Dewey Bridge, Utah, is one of the longest navigable waterways in the continental United States. Except when it isn't. Throughout many summers, the stream's voice had weakened to a mumble. Its flow was too meager to even buoy a duck—the result of drought and a dam diverting most of its lifeblood for irrigation. In the spring of 2005 the spell finally broke. Unexpected snowfalls in the southern Rockies combined with soaring May temperatures had the Dolores showing true grit again.

It is early in the season, as we are reminded the morning after our four rafts pulled away from the Slick Rock launch site. The canyon's hulk and the crisp high-desert air drive us to huddle in a broadening wedge of sunlight on the beach. Hesitant to face the cold water just yet, we go for a hike instead. After much trial and error we piece together a route through rock balconies receding above camp until, at last, we top out on the canyon's lip. Sunlit capstone outlines curves still draped in shadows, while the La Sal Mountains bridge the western horizon—a snowy mirage.

Perhaps as a consequence of low visitation during previous years, a re-wilding of the river corridor has taken place. Some campsites marked on our map no longer exist; tamarisk, scrub oak, reeds, willows, and box elders have reclaimed them. We glide by beavers and muskrats snug in their dens in the riverbank. Bull and garter snakes abound. An ancient cottonwood tree at Mile 140 hosts six heron nests guarded by twice as many stoic birds. We spot bald eagles, and at some point, peregrines greet us by screeching from their cliff aerie. Near Bedrock two elk cows and a bull attempt to ford the river in front of my kayak. Spooked by my seesawing paddle or scent, they turn back, crashing through the gallery forest. To them our playground is home.

Mount Tukuhnikivats

THE PEAK WITH the tongue-twisting name floats 12,482 feet above Moab, crowded by a handful of summits that fall just short of the 13,000-foot mark. A refuge on hot summer days it hosts alpine plants commonly found at Canadian latitudes. Tukuhnikivats forms the centerpiece of the Sierra de la Sal, the range a Spanish expedition named in 1776. Salt deposits in the region, which are responsible for alkaline creeks—and indirectly for arches and paradox valleys—inspired the Spaniards in their christening. Paiute Indians already knew this place as Where the Light Lingers, and the soft play of alpenglow on wintry heights proves the name's propriety. In town, tourists long for the bold slopes and ridgelines that may be snow-free only between June and October.

Near the top, hikers built a rock enclosure to hide from sharp winds. A shingled rib hitches the summit to Tukno, a storm-battered knoll. The subaltern peak opens views onto unruly desert sprawling below, and no greater geological contrast can be imagined. Whereas Canyonlands' belted turrets testify to an evenness of deposition throughout the ages, Tukuhnikivats owes its rugged looks to subterranean tremors. Like the Henry Mountains to the west and Navajo Mountain farther south, the La Sals straddle a volcanic blister in Earth's hide. As magma squeezed from the planet's fiery core and met more resistant rock, it mushroomed into a cap of gigantic dimensions. Lodged at shallow depths these intrusions can bloom to more than five miles in diameter and be half a mile thick. They bucked overlying layers into a dome, which weather and gravity continue to work into rubble and bring down.

As I descend Tukuhnikivats' shoulder, nature announces its grand scheme in more intimate ways. From among rock debris a pika whistles, preparing for fall, urging me to hurry. Pink cotton-candy clouds have already obliterated the summit. Daisies bunch low against acres of scree. My shadow stretches behind me, a silent doppelganger, a perfect hiking companion. Haze drapes the valley in purple, and—trembling like stars—town lights guide me toward home.

Comb Ridge

ABOUT FIFTEEN MILES from Natural Bridges, where tablelands tilt nearly upright, Highway 95 punches through a ramp of Jurassic bedrock that runs ninety miles north to south. Resemblance to a rooster's scalloped headgear suggested the name for this crest. Its undulations afford expansive views, a panorama encompassing some classic landforms of the Four Corners region. To the north the Abajo Mountains serrate the horizon; due south the San Juan River wends its way past the hamlet of Bluff; east of the parapet Cedar Mesa's high piñon-juniper country stews in midsummer haze; and lost in the pearly distance, spires and buttes delineate Monument Valley, perhaps the Southwest's most-photogenic landscape. Diné stories recount how a mythical hero created Comb Ridge and its parallel wash after he slew a monster: he scraped a furrow into the dirt to prevent the creature's poisonous blood from reaching him.

Geologists tell different stories. In their worldview, monoclines like Comb Ridge separate the margins of uplifts from adjacent basins and are a trademark of the Colorado Plateau. Compression pried blocks of Earth's rind upward while neighboring blocks sank. Deep-seated faults buried under sediment seam the desert like poorly healed sutures. Runoff scoured Comb Ridge, the San Rafael Swell, Waterpocket Fold, and similar upheavals, giving birth to narrow and secluded rifts.

We are camped on a ledge in the lee of the ridge, warming our hands on mugs of steaming tea. About three feet from our tent the ground pitches into a precipice. We watch as a sea of fog pours in from the San Juan River, blotting out Moenkopi badlands 600 feet below. Soon the silent tide washes against the escarpment's western base. For a while the highest promontories stay afloat, gilded by a dying sun. Eventually the flood succeeds; it wells up naked flanks, spills over, and sweeps onward as if on fast-forward. The world turns colder the moment sunlight slips off its rim.

We retire early. Cocooned in our tent, we listen to coyotes yodeling in the plains.

Bowknot Bend

"ABOUT SIX MILES below noon camp we go around a great bend to the right, five miles in length and come back to a point within a quarter mile of where we started. Then we sweep around another great bend to the left, making a circuit of nine miles and come back to a point within 600 feet of the beginning of the bend. In the two circuits we describe almost the figure 8. The men call it a 'bowknot' of a river; so we name it Bowknot Bend."

What sounds like the description of a gigantic Moebius strip or a roller coaster ride is actually Major John Wesley Powell's account of a meander in the Green River's Labyrinth Canyon. Named after a river in Greece, meanders are typical of streams with low gradients. Where the underlying rock strata are friable and homogenous, whorls of a tipsy watercourse burrow deep into the land. Though lacking in rapids or falls, the stretch between Interstate 70 and the confluence of the Colorado and Green is one of the last wild river runs of the West. Flaring Navajo sandstone, solitude, and scores of enchanted side canyons make it a paradise for canoeists and campers alike. A dam was planned at Bowknot Bend and uranium once mined on its eastern banks. Yet it still harbors undisturbed desert flora; the spur that connects mesa with mainland is crumbling, and therefore cattle have never grazed its top. The river will eventually churn through this gooseneck, creating a direct route and leaving the meander dried-up, abandoned—a Rincon.

A half-hour climb up the saddle leads to the River Post Office, a register where boaters leave their names or messages for parties en route to Cataract Canyon. But most venture there for the sweeping view. In vertiginous symmetry the flood rubs against both sides of the isthmus like a ginger cat, coming *and* going. You find yourself upstream and downstream at once. Bench lands wheel about, while a robin-egg sky arches above everything.

Cataract Canyon

THE INSTANT MY fourteen-foot raft dips into a gnarly hydraulic on the left side of Rapid No. 5 I realize I will not make it. Before I can so much as yell "high-side!" to have my sole passenger balance the boat, it flips, and the maelstrom sucks me under. Crosscurrents tumble me like laundry in a dryer. I cannot tell up from down. Eternities later, I am pardoned and ascend toward diffuse light. I surface, sputtering. After assuring myself that my companion is alive and clinging to the rubber hull, we pull the raft into an eddy to right it.

A little ways below the confluence of the Colorado and Green rivers that worm their way into Canyonlands National Park, a sign warns boaters of hazards downstream. Three and a half miles from the junction, the middle-aged river throws itself with renewed vigor into whirlpools and over drops, against house rocks and headwalls, battling confinement. Its convulsions splinter driftwood and oars as carelessly as the egos of confident boaters. The same rapids tested Major Powell and his crew, who acknowledged the stream's clout with the name Cataract Canyon.

I find myself part of a long tradition. Near Rapid No. 15, an inscription pecked into a varnished boulder by the Best expedition of 1891 speaks volumes: Camp #7, Hell to Pay, No. 1 Sunk & Down. "No. 1" was half of this mining outfit's miserable fleet of wooden tubs. A purported Grand Canyon ledge of pure silver they were chasing turned out to be nothing but mica and schist—fools' dreams glittering in the sun.

These days, with Glen Canyon Reservoir depleted by drought, two major rapids that were formerly washed out have come to life again, adding to the twenty-five marked on river maps. Along this whitewater gauntlet, three "big drops" challenge river runners. With its rapids, its limestone narrows, marine fossils of stromatolites and shells, and sets of forked tributaries, Cataract Canyon provides enough thrills for a lifetime. Just be sure to bring a life jacket.

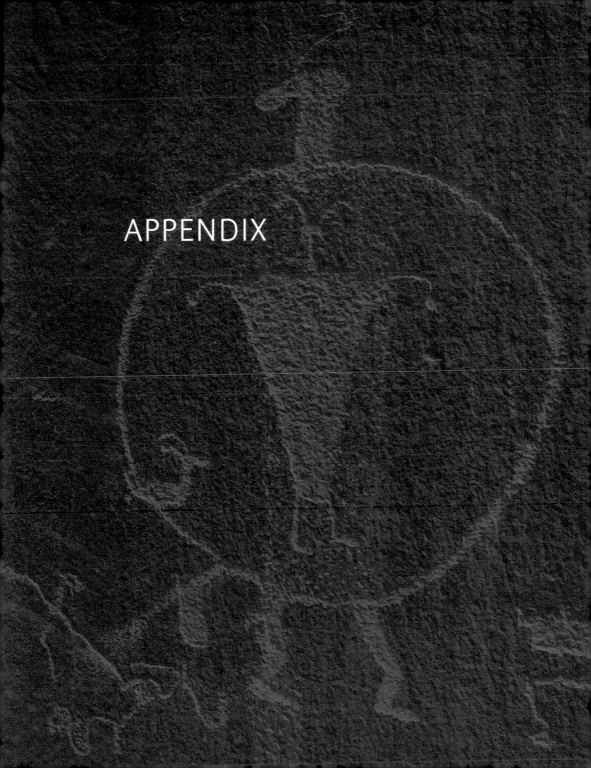

APPENDIX

SUGGESTED READING

Baars, Donald L. *The Colorado Plateau: A Geologic History*. Albuquerque: University of New Mexico Press, 2000.

Fagan, Damian. *Canyon Country Wildflowers: Including Arches and Canyonlands National Park*. Helena, Mont.: Falcon, 1998.

Friederici, Peter, ed. *Earth Notes: Exploring the Southwest's Canyon Country from the Airwaves*. Flagstaff, Ariz.: Grand Canyon Association and KNAU, 2005.

Harper, Kimball, et. al., ed. *Natural History of the Colorado Plateau and Great Basin*. Niwot, Colo.: University Press of Colorado, 1994.

Kluckhohn, Clyde, and Dorothea Leighton. *The Navajo*. New York: Doubleday, 1962.

Martineau, Lavan. *Southern Paiutes: Legends, Lore, Language and Lineage*. Las Vegas: KC Publishing, 1992.

McPherson, Robert S. *Sacred Land, Sacred View: Navajo Perceptions of the Four Corners Region*. Salt Lake City: Brigham Young University Press, 1992.

Patterson, Alex. *A Field Guide to Rock Art Symbols of the Greater Southwest*. Boulder, Colo.: Johnson Books, 1992.

Roberts, David. *In Search of the Old Ones: Exploring the Anasazi World of the Southwest*. New York: Simon & Schuster, 1997.

Sadler, Christa. *Life in Stone: Fossils of the Colorado Plateau*. Grand Canyon, Ariz.: Grand Canyon Association, 2005.

Tweit, Susan. *The Great Southwest Nature Factbook: A Guide to the Region's Remarkable Animals, Plants, and Natural Features*. Seattle: Alaska Northwest Books, 1992.

Whitney, Stephen. *A Field Guide to the Grand Canyon*. Seattle: Mountaineers Books, 1996.

Williams, David B. *A Naturalist's Guide to Canyon Country*. Helena, Mont.: Falcon, 2000.

CONTACTS

Peaks, Plateaus & Canyons Association is a consortium of 14 cooperating associations on the Colorado Plateau. Your purchase from a non-profit cooperating association bookstore helps to support the public lands you are visiting. To find out more, visit PPCA's Web site www.ppca.org.

Arizona Natural History Association
(928) 527-3450
www.aznaturalhistory.org

Arizona Strip Interpretive Association
(435) 688-3275
www.azstrip.az.blm.gov

Bryce Canyon Natural History Association
(435) 834-4600
www.brycecanyon.org

Canyonlands Natural History Association
(435) 259-6003
www.chna.org

Capitol Reef Natural History Association
(435) 425-3791 ext. 115
www.capitolreef.org

Colorado National Monument Association
(970) 858-3617
www.coloradonma.org

Glen Canyon Natural History Association
(928) 608-6358
www.GlenCanyonNHA.org

Grand Canyon Association
(928) 638-2481
www.grandcanyon.org

Mesa Verde Museum Association
(970) 529-4445
www.mesaverde.org

Peaks, Plateaus & Canyons Association
(435) 259-6003 ext. 13
www.ppcaweb.org

Petrified Forest Museum Association
(928) 524-6228 ext. 239
www.cybertrails.com/~pfma

Western National Parks Association
(520) 622-1999
www.wpna.org

Zion Natural History Association
(435) 772-3265 or 3264
www.zionpark.org

PHOTO CREDITS

John Blaustein *98*
    © 2006 from *The Hidden Canyon: A River Journey*

Bob Cameron *author photo, 100*

Lynn Chamberlain *back cover, 50, 54, 58*

James Crotty *24*

Dean Cully *104*

Dreamstime *46, 48, 56*

Kevin Ebi *34*

Michael Engelhard *8, 26, 40*

Melissa Guy *86*

Melissa Hutchison *94*

Joel D. Lusk *60*

Steve MacAulay *22*

Tony Markle *64*

Markus Mauthe *6, 10, 42*

Suzi Moore McGregor *XIII*

Mike Morrison *front cover (sandstone), VI-VII, 4*

H. Scott Page *52*

Photo.com *44*

Andrew Reitsma *62*

John Running *66, 84*

Tom Till *front cover (cactus blossom), II, VIII-IX, XIV, 2, 12, 14, 16, 18, 20*
    28, 30, 32, 36, 38, 68, 70, 72, 74, 76,
    78, 80, 82, 88, 90, 92, 96, 102, 106, 108, 110